Adventure Walks
for Little Explorers

The Yorkshire Dales

Adventure Walks
for Little Explorers

The Yorkshire Dales

Rebecca Chippindale and Rebecca Terry

Published by Sigma Leisure – an imprint of
Sigma Press, Stobart House, Pontyclerc, Penybanc Road
Ammanford, Carmarthenshire SA18 3HP

British Library Cataloguing in Publication Data

A CIP record for this book is available from the British Library

ISBN: 978-1-85058-897-9

Typesetting and Design by: Sigma Press, Ammanford, Wales

Cover Photograph: Phillip Elsdon

Maps: Rebecca Terry

Photographs: Rebecca Chippindale and Phillip Elsdon

Printed by: TJ International Ltd

Disclaimer: The information in this book is given in good faith and is believed to be correct at the time of publication. Care should always be taken when walking in hill country. Where appropriate, attention has been drawn to matters of safety. The author and publisher cannot take responsibility for any accidents or injury incurred whilst following these walks. Only you can judge your own fitness, competence and experience. Do not rely solely on sketch maps for navigation: we strongly recommend the use of appropriate Ordnance Survey (or equivalent) maps.

Preface

The Yorkshire Dales is such a vast and wonderful landscape. It encompasses all kinds of terrain and scenery from woods to waterfalls, farmland and moorland, druids temples, abbeys, reservoirs, rivers and much more in between.

While we, as adults can appreciate all this, the idea behind 'Adventure Walks for Little Explorers' is to bring the countryside to life for children - to turn a walk into an adventure, making it fun and fascinating. Our aim is to give you some good tools for cajoling those who might not (yet) be as keen as the grown-ups to get outdoors for some fresh air and exercise...

With this in mind, each of the fifteen walks has a checklist which is split into four parts – Spot, Feel, Magnify, Collect. Some have a few facts tagged on and all walks include a suggestion for a post-walk activity and at least one suggestion for something else to do in the area.

We would love to have been able to include a special kit with this book (with a magnifying glass, collectors bag, some crayons etc), but decided most households would have at least some of these things to hand. The only thing we would really recommend buying, if you do not already have one, is a basic magnifying glass.

We have completed all these walks ourselves – with our children; so we know they are do-able. We realize that not all the activities will appeal to each individual child and that you may not even feel like doing them yourself! They are just a guide or idea to keep things moving...

Acknowledgements

Thanks to Sam, Emma and Emily for coming on all these walks with us – and to Jamie and Molly for joining us in the school holidays. Also, a big thank you to our 'other halves' for surviving the camping trip. Mr Bond, your patience was most appreciated; and Phil, the roast was exemplary…

Contents

Introduction   9

The Countryside Code   11

Walk location map   12

Key to walk symbols   13

The Walks

Walk 1: Dent   15
Distance: 3 miles, Time: 1hr 30 mins, Grade: Easy

Walk 2: Aysgarth Falls   20
Distance: 1.4 miles, Time: 1hr, Grade: Moderate

Walk 3: Masham   26
Distance: 3.3 miles, Time: 2hrs, Grade: Moderate

Walk 4: Ribblehead Viaduct   32
Distance: 2.6 miles, Time: 1hr 30mins, Grade: Moderate

Walk 5: Druids Temple, Ilton   37
Distance: 1 mile, Time: 1hr 30 mins, Grade: Easy

Walk 6: Stainforth (Catrigg Force)   42
Distance: 2.25 miles, Time: 1hr 45mins, Grade: Hard

Walk 7: Settle   48
Distance: 3.2 miles, Time: 2hrs, Grade: Moderate

Walk 8: Malham   54
Distance: 2.3 miles, Time: 1hr 30mins, Grade: Moderate

Walk 9: Grassington   60
Distance: 2.2 miles, Time: 1hr 30mins, Grade: Moderate

Walk 10: Pateley Bridge   66
Distance: 1.9 miles, Time: 1hr 15mins, Grade: Easy

Walk 11: Ripley Castle Perimeter   71
Distance: 2.9 miles, Time: 2hrs, Grade: Easy

Walk 12: Skipton Woods   76
Distance: 2.3 miles, Time: 1hr 30mins, Grade: Hard

Walk 13: Bolton Abbey   81
Distance: 2.1 miles, Time: 1hr 30mins, Grade: Moderate

Walk 14: Lindley Wood Reservoir   86
Distance: 2.3 miles, Time: 2hrs, Grade: Easy

Walk 15: Middleton Woods, Ilkley   91
Distance: 0.9 miles, Time: 1hr, Grade: Moderate

Post Walk Activities

  1: **Edible sheep**   96
  2: **Leaf collage**   99
  3: **Decorated eggs**   101
  4: **Chalk drawing**   103
  5: **Conkers**   105
  6: **Stone bugs**   106
  7: **Pine cone bird feeder**   108
  8: **Dinosaur footprints**   109
  9: **Yorkshire rose flag**   111
 10: **Krispie birds nests**   112
 11: **Cardboard castle**   114
 12: **Clock face**   116
 13: **St. George's flag collage**   118
 14. **Blackberry and banana muffins**   120
 15: **Twig photo frame**   122
 16. **How to play Poohsticks**   124
 17. **Pond dipping**   125
 18. **Crayon rubbings**   127

Introduction

We have tried to include a wide variety of landscapes and terrains in this book and, where possible, have chosen circular rather than there-and-back routes.

As with our previous series (*All-Terrain Pushchair Walks*), we have used simple symbols at the top of each walk, making it quick and easy to choose one to suit your mood, ability and time scale.

A short paragraph follows the symbols with more details and facts about the area. Then there's the 'post-walk activity', plus a list of anything extra which you may need to take with you.

You will also find Ordnance Survey references, directions and a suggestion for parking. We have taken the broad view that most of our readers will have travelled by car to reach the starting point.

The paragraph numbers correspond to the numbers on the map, to make it easy to follow.

Be Prepared
As with any walk with children, being prepared is key to a successful day out.

Here's a list of things you might want to consider taking with you, other than the suggested bits and pieces at the beginning of each walk.

To work with alongside the book:
- Magnifying glass
- Plastic carrier bag / small Tupperware (to collect things in)
- Wipes for after 'feeling' things and/or a small towel
- Pencil/pen to tick things off the checklist

In General:
- Some cash for car parking/cafés etc
- Picnic / drinks / treats

- Spare clothes
- Cagool/wellingtons/hats and gloves
- Sun hat/suncream/sunglasses
- Mobile phone
  Small first aid kit
  This book for the directions
  Ordnance Survey Map

Rebecca Chippindale
Rebecca Terry

The Countryside Code

Respect – Protect – Enjoy

- Do not drop litter. Use a bin or take it home

- Do not stray from public footpaths or bridleways

- Do not pick any plants

- Make no unnecessary noise

- Keep dogs on a lead near livestock and under close control at all other times

- Leave gates as you find them

- Use gates or stiles to cross fences, hedges or walls

- Do not touch livestock, crops or farm machinery

- Keep the natural water supply clean

- Walk in single file and on the right hand side of roads

- Do not cross railway lines except by bridges

- Guard against the risk of fire.

For information on new access rights, visit
www.countysideaccess.gov.uk or phone 0845 100 3298

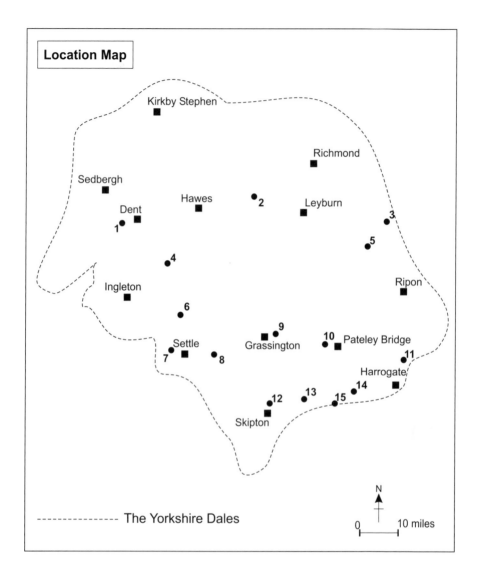

Location Map

Kirkby Stephen

Richmond

Sedbergh

Hawes
2
Leyburn
3

Dent
1

5

4

Ingleton

Ripon

6

9
10 Pateley Bridge
Settle
Grassington
11
7
8
Harrogate
14
12 13 15
Skipton

N

-------- The Yorkshire Dales

0   10 miles

Key to walk symbols.

Circular route.

There and back. Route is non-circular.

Easy route with very few hills.

Moderate exertion. Some gentle ascents and descents.

Hard going. Route incorporates some steep inclines.

Easy terrain, trainers suitable.

Muddy and wet. Wellington boots or hiking boots are required.

Rough terrain. Rocky and uneven ground, hiking boots recommended.

Stile

Icecream van on route!

Tea shop.

Pub/Hotel.

Picnic table.

Children's play ground

Trains.

Ducks!

Toilets.

Solo. Walk can be accomplished alone.

At least two people required to complete walk. Pushchair may need to be lifted over obstacles.

Money required for parking, entrance fee or rail fare.

Walk 1: Dent

       £

Dent is a pretty village in the valley of Dentdale – with lovely cobbled streets, stone cottages and the River Dee running through it. It was the birthplace of the famous geologist Adam Sedgwick (you will pass his statue on the return leg of this walk). Out of the village, the landscape is a real mixture of Lakeland Fells and rolling hills. This walk basically takes you along the River Dee in one direction, and back along the other side. There are a handful of good cafés and pubs in Dent – as well as an excellent Heritage Centre.

Distance	3 miles (4.8 km)
Allow	1 hour 30 minutes
Take with you	Small bag for collectables, magnifying glass, something to put blackberries in if it is blackberry-picking season
Getting there and parking	Take the turning for Dent from the B6255 between Hawes and Ribblehead. Follow this long winding road all the way to the village (not the station). Park in the Dentdale Pay & Display car park (just opposite the National School 1945)
Map	Ordnance Survey Explorer OL2
Grid Reference	704871
Post walk activity	Create an Edible Sheep when you return home (see Activity 1 on page 96)

Dent Checklist

Spot

- ☐ The Age of the National school
- ☐ Tents
- ☐ Sign saying 'Winter Food for Livestock'
- ☐ Swaledale sheep (one with curly horns)
- ☐ Tractor
- ☐ Fish in the river
- ☐ Rock saying 'Adam Sedgwick – father of geology'
- ☐ Dog gate (looks like a flattened cricket bat)

Feel

Rosehip. Just touch the leafy part and the outside of the red pod. The inside of the pod is very itchy, so don't break it open. Does the pod feel smooth? How about the bits on the end of the pods – they look a bit crispy – is that how they feel? Did you know that rose hips are used for all sorts of things? They can be used in jam, tea and even soup. Rose hips also have medicinal purposes – some say it can help with colds or even rheumatoid arthritis.

Magnify

Clover – can you find one with four leaves? According to legend, if you find a four leaf clover, you will have good luck as each leaf represents something: The first is hope, the second is faith, the third is love and the fourth is luck. Apparently, there is roughly one four-leafed clover in every ten thousand with three leaves!

Collect

Blackberries (if in season) to eat along the way

Start at the entrance of the car park and turn right. This little road takes you past some lovely cottages. Opposite the sign for High Laning Farm, there is a green gate on the right hand side. Follow the sign which says 'FP's River Dee, Back Lane'. This takes you down a path between the terraced houses and very shortly, a campsite on the left.

After a short while, you will go through another gate. Follow this path down with the wall on your right hand side. Then you will come to a kissing gate – go through this and follow it round to the right. Almost immediately you will see another small wooden gate – go through that one too, then turn left heading towards the big hill in front.

1. Keep on this path until you reach another kissing gate – go through it and keep to the path with the wall on your left. Eventually you will reach the river. Cross over the wooden stile and turn left. Just keep to the footpath with the river on your right.

   When you get to another wooden gate – go through it and if it's summertime, you will see tents on the left hand side. The river will still be on the right. Then you will reach some cobbles, then a black

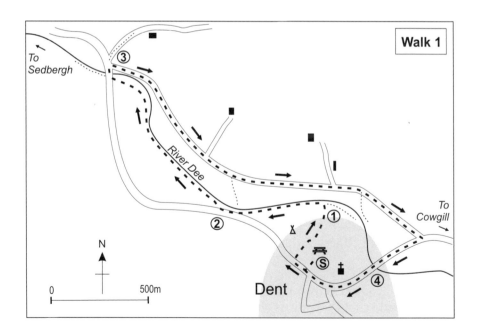

Adam Sedgwick Rock in Dent village

kissing gate. Go through the kissing gate and stick to the path. This brings you out onto the road, where you need to turn right.

2. Very shortly on your right hand side you will see another black kissing gate. Go through this to take you back off the road again. You will also see a sign which says 'Barth Bridge ½ miles'. Keep to this path with the river on your right.

Then you come to another wooden footpath gate – go through it and keep straight ahead. Eventually you will come to a little wooden footbridge – go over that, then through one wooden gate and then immediately over a tiny stone footbridge – then through another wooden gate. Keep to this path with the river still on your right.

After a while you will reach a black metal kissing gate and a couple of stone steps. Go through the gate and over a little stone footpath and head straight towards the next gate.

Go through that wooden gate and into a field. Keep straight ahead where you will see another wooden gate, which you need to go through, then up some stone steps. This takes you to the bridge. Turn right, so you are crossing over the river on the bridge.

3. At the end of the bridge, turn immediate right onto a little tarmac road with the river on your right. You are now half way into the walk. So, stick to this road for a long time until you reach a junction. Turn right at the junction following signs for 'Dent and Sedbergh' – along the road and over the bridge.

4. You will soon see a Dent Sign – follow that up. You will also see the church too. This road takes you into the village, so just keep following it round until you get to the car park on the right hand side.

In the area
If you like music and beer, you should come here at the end of June – check out the website **www.dentmusicandbeer.com** which has details of a summer festival. Or why not rest your weary legs and catch the Settle to Carlsile train at Dent station and take in some of the beautiful scenery? Ticket prices and timetables can be found at **www.settle-carlsile.co.uk** or by using the freephone number 0800 980 0766.

Walk 2: Aysgarth Falls

Aysgarth Falls is one of Wenslydales' most famous beauty spots – so much so that it was included in Kevin Kostners' film 'Robin Hood, Prince of Thieves'. But it's not just known for its beauty… The area is now Site of Specific Scientific Interest and a Nature Reserve – with a rich array of British trees grown there (Hazel being the main one) and around one hundred and twenty species of flower. It's particularly beautiful when all the bluebells and woodland daisies are out.

Aysgarth Falls

Distance	1.4 miles (2.3 km)
Allow	1 hour
Take with you	Crayon and paper, towel for drying toes after paddling, small bag for collectables, magnifying glass
Getting there and parking	Aysgarth is situated on the A684 between Bainbridge and Leyburn. Take the turning towards Carperby from Aysgarth following the signs for the National Park Centre (Aysgarth Falls). Park in the National Park pay and display car park
Map	Ordnance Survey Explorer OL30
Grid Reference	012887
Post walk activity	Make a collage with crayon rubbings made from various carvings you will pass along the way. Or mix them up in a collage with other bits of nature collected en route (feathers, leaves etc). See Activity 2 on page 99; and Activty 18 on page 127 for details of how to do crayon rubbings.

There are three main waterfalls, which through time have been carved out of the River Ure. This walk covers two of the waterfalls with a third option at the end (depending on how the children are doing). The Yorkshire Dales National Park Centre has a host of information about the history of the area, as well as a lovely café with seating inside and out and gift shop. You will also notice something slightly unusual about the toilets...

Leave the car park by the main exit, heading towards the middle and lower falls, keeping to the footpath as it veers round right. Cross over the road at the bottom, go through the wooden gate and keep to the

Aysgarth Falls Checklist

Spot

☐ Stuffed fox
☐ Wooden bench with three steps (what does it say on them?)
☐ St Andrews Church
☐ Writing on some steps 'hard limestone'
☐ Fish carved into a handrail
☐ Swamp/Bog
☐ Squirrel
☐ Kissing gate

Feel

Swaledale Ram head sculpture. Can you feel how the wood has been cut into? Is it nice and smooth or rough? Is it wet or dry?

Magnify

Holly bush. Can you see any veins on the leaves? Are they all the same colour green or different shades? Are there any red berries? Did you know there are about four hundred different species of holly? *Ilex Aquifolium* is the name given to the main type of holly grown in Britain (the one generally used in Christmas decorations), which translated, literally means 'needle leaf'.

Collect

Keep hold of all your rubbings from various carvings throughout the walk. Also, see if you can pick anything up which might look interesting in a collage, such as leaves, small pine cones, etc.

path. You will see a sign saying 'Freeholders Wood and Widdings Field' (local Nature Reserve). Follow the footpath signs to 'Lower and Middle Falls' 400 yards.

1. Soon you will reach a signpost for 'Middle Falls' (number two trail stop). Go down the steps to have a look at the waterfall and view, then come straight back up again (looking carefully at the writing on the steps and handrail) to rejoin the path.

    There are a lot of small trails off to the left and right, but stick to the main path. You will still be able to see the children if they venture onto these other paths. Eventually you will come to three gates next to each other – a kissing gate and two wooden ones. Go through the kissing gate and stick straight to this path, following signs to 'Lower Falls'. Look out for the rams head!

2. Shortly you will see a big grassy mound with a mud path up it – a good place to race to the top and look at the views. When you've

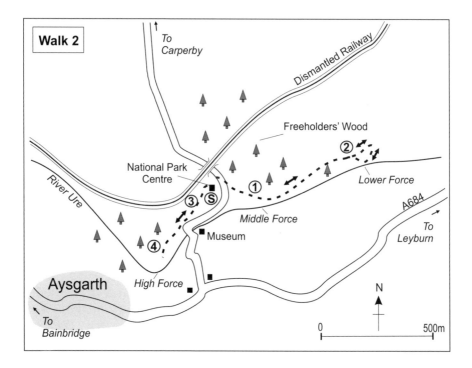

done that, come back down and rejoin the path. Eventually you will reach some steps and a gate. Go through the gate, head down the 'Lower Falls Viewing Point'. You should be able to hear the waterfalls form here.

You will see some stones which start with the words 'Three hundred million years ago....'. Just stick to this path until it brings you out to the falls at the end. If your children are prone to running off ahead, it might be an idea to keep up with them along here as there is no fence in front of the waterfall! This is a lovely place to paddle – especially in the more shallow areas slightly further up.

You will see a sign for 'Return Path', which takes you up some steps through the trees. When you get to the top, go through a wooden gate, up the steps and turn left (rejoining the main path). Stick to this route until you reach the three gates again.

Go through the kissing gate and keep going on this path, right to the top, passing one set of gates to the left (opposite Number One Trail stop). Just past this gate you will see the original gate which you came through at the beginning of the walk. Go back through this gate and cross over the road, rejoining the path back up to the car park.

3. To extend this walk a little further, you could include the High Falls now. To do this, head out of the car park in the other direction (i.e. with the National Park Centre and exit behind you), and take a left, downhill. You will eventually see a Mill and a bridge on the left hand side. Keep to the path and go through the wooden gate, following signs for 'Upper Falls and Picnic Area'.

4. You will come to two wooden gates. Go through the higher one which says 'Entrance' and then follow the path round to the right. To the left you will see Upper Falls. This is another good spot for paddling.

When you have finished here, literally turn around and head back in the direction you came, leading you up to the car park and National Park Centre.

In the area

Wenslydale Creameries, Gayle Lane, Hawes, DL8 3RN. Go and see how Wensleydale cheese is made and visit their specialist cheese shop or (licensed) restaurant. Ring or email first to check opening times: Tel: 01969 667 664 **www.wensleydale.co.uk**

Walk 3: Masham

     £

Masham is a lovely little market town in Wenslydale, surrounded by beautiful Georgian houses. The church, St Mary's, was founded in the seventh century and is the final resting place for artists Julius Caesar Ibbotson and George Cuit. There are many walks around this area, but we chose this one around Marfield Nature Reserve as it offers quite a variety of 'spotting' opportunities for the children. Depending on the time of year, you may come across all kinds of flora and fauna – from simple snowdrops to yellow aconites, hazel catkins or even oak apples and ivy berries.

Distance	3.3 miles (5.3km)
Allow	2 hours (more if stopping for a picnic)
Take with you	A bit of extra cash if you fancy buying some free range eggs on the walk (for decorating as part of the post-walk activity), magnifying glass, an apple or carrot for the horses
Getting there and parking	Park in the Market Square. There is an honesty box with a recommended donation of fifty pence
Map	Ordnance Survey Explorer 302
Grid Reference	224807
Post walk activity	Decorating a hard boiled egg (which may have been bought from the farm which you will pass on the return leg of the walk). See Activity 3 on page 101

After parking, turn to face the shop called Joneva. Just to your left and ahead across the road, you will see Aura Antique shop on Silver Street. Cross over the road towards the Antique shop and head down Silver Street away from the Market Square towards the Post Office.

1. Veer left past Honeysuckle Cottage, towards Hodgsons Ltd. At the junction, cross straight over the road onto another junction towards the Black Sheep Brewery Visitor Centre and keep to this pavement. You will pass The White Bear Hotel on your right, then the Black Sheep Brewery (also on your right).

   This road turns a bit more rural – keep going on this public bridleway past some farm buildings. When you reach a metal gate, go through it and veer left. Before you get to the cattle grid, turn right and follow the fence on your left hand side along the field.

2. Go through the next metal gate and turn left. Before long you will see the main road ahead. Before you get to the main road, turn off right towards a wooden fence/gate on the grass (and the Public Bridleway sign). Go through this and stick to the path. It gets quite muddy along here so be careful. Along this path you will see what looks like some large ponds to the right. They are old gravel pits (Marfield Gravel Pits) which is now Marfield Nature Reserve. There are also loads of blackberry bushes on the left of this path if you are feeling peckish.

3. This path looks like it comes to a dead end. Instead of turning left towards the main road, follow the footpath arrow right, which follows the edge of the Nature Reserve. You will pass a bench on the left and eventually come to a bird hide. Keep to this path which soon opens out onto a small car park. You will see a quarry straight ahead. Go to the exit of the car park and turn right along the path/road.

4. Just before you reach a cattle grid, there is a double metal gate on your right which takes you back into the Marfield Wetlands. Go through this and head down and left off the path towards a kissing gate (signposted). When you are through the gate head across the field towards the top right of the lake where you will

Masham Checklist

Spot

- ☐ Old Cross
- ☐ Honesty box
- ☐ Church clock
- ☐ Fish door knocker (on Silver Street)
- ☐ Shetland ponies
- ☐ Rabbits
- ☐ Lake
- ☐ Geese
- ☐ Tractor

Feel

If the horses are near the fence, stroke their faces very gently. See how the fur in the middle of their noses is coarser than nearer the nostrils – and more bristly near the chin. You might be able to tempt one over with a carrot or apple. Please do not feed them though if there is a notice advising against this

Magnify

Molehill. Other than soil what can you see? Are there any earthworms or insect larvae (a moles favourite food)? Molehills are basically just waste soil dug up when moles are either creating new holes or repairing old ones. Molehills are very good for the soil as they help aerate it, which in turn makes the soil more fertile. Did you know that an adult mole will eat about half its body weight in food per day? That's a lot of earthworms!

Collect

Free range eggs and feathers for the post-walk activity

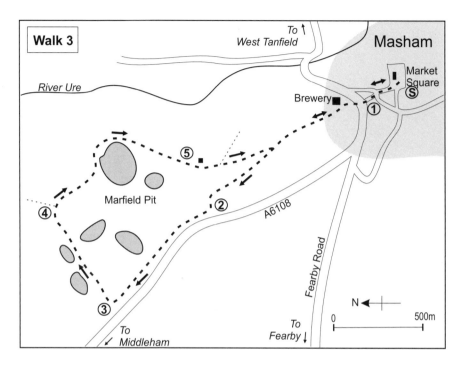

come across the footpath arrow again. Follow this footpath. You will pass a bench and eventually come to another bird hide on your left.

5. The path opens up. Keep going straight ahead towards a metal gate. You will see a few houses to your left and, if you are lucky, there might be some free range eggs for sale on a table nearby (handy for the activity when you get home). Go through the gate and follow the road ahead. Not long after the road straightens out, you will see a wooden gate on your left with a public footpath arrow on it. Go through the gate and go straight ahead over the field towards a stile.

Go over the stile and keep straight ahead. You will see the church in the distance. When you get to the small tarmac road in front of the farm, cross over it and go through the metal gate which says public bridleway and has a blue arrow on it. You should now recognise where you are.

Marfield Nature Reserve (taken from inside the bird hide)

Keep straight on this path, (passing the Black Sheep Brewery and White Bear Hotel again) until you get to the junction of the main road. Cross over to the other side, re-joining Silver Street and keep going until you reach the Antique shop on your right, with the Market Square in front of you. Cross over the road to the Market Square and you are back to the beginning.

In the Area

For beer lovers, there are two breweries based in Masham – Black Sheep and Theakstons – both of which have visitors centres. The Black Sheep brewery offers tours, where you can see how the beer is made from start to finish (and then sample a bit – over 18's only for the sampling...). Black Sheep Brewery, Wellgarth, Masham, Ripon, HG4 4EN. Ring first to check opening times: 01756 680 100. Or visit their website **www.blacksheepbrewery.com**.

Or, depending on how much you want to cram into your day, there's also Fountains Abbey and Studley Royal, Ripon, HG4 3DY. It is a world heritage site with eight hundred acres and 12th Centrury ruins of the Abbey. There's a medieval deer park, with over five hundred deer, Georgian water gardens and neo-classical statues. If you're going during school holidays, take advantage of the free trails and craft workshops. To check opening times and prices Tel: 01756 608 888 or visit their website: **www.fountainsabbey.org.uk**.

Walk 4: Ribblehead Viaduct

This walk takes you underneath the longest and most famous viaduct on the Settle-Carlisle Railway. Situated at the foot of Whernside, the viaduct stands at an impressive 104 feet high. Its' twenty four arches were designed by engineer John Sydney Crossley. Starting in October 1870, his project took hundreds of men four years to complete. If your little one is into Thomas the Tank engine, you might want to know that

Distance	2.6 miles (4.2 km)
Allow	1 hour 30 minutes
Take with you	Magnifying glass, towel for drying toes after a paddle, some money to 'collect' an ice cream at the end
Getting there and parking	Ribblehead is situated at the junction of the B6479 (Settle) and the B6255 (Ingleton to Hawes). Park opposite the Station Inn pub at Ribblehead
Map	Ordnance Survey Explorer OL2
Grid Reference	764792
Post walk activity	A chalk drawing of something you remember from the walk – perhaps the viaduct? This is to link in with the limestone rock facts. See Activity 4 on page 103

this viaduct featured in the film 'Thomas and the Magic Railroad'. However, in the film, this viaduct collapses... The terrain is a rough mix of Limestone and moorland path.

This is a steady walk with lots of wide open space and plenty of opportunities to stop for picnics.

Walk down hill towards a cattle grid, passing the Station Inn Bunk Barn on your left. Go through the wooden gate next to the cattle grid and cross the road to follow the footpath signed 'Whernside 4½ miles'.

1. This path takes you underneath the viaduct. Keep straight ahead, ignoring the path which veers to the right. Eventually you will get to a big metal gate – go through it and keep straight ahead. You will pass some farm buildings on your right.

    Walk over the bridge and turn right onto the little lane (so the stream is now on your right). Whernside mountain is visible to the left.

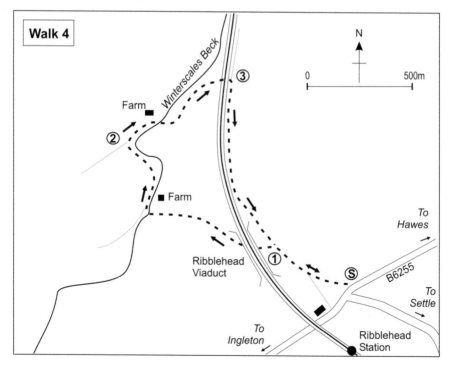

Ribblehead Viaduct Checklist

Spot

- ☐ 24 arches
- ☐ Whernside mountain
- ☐ Ice cream van
- ☐ Sheep
- ☐ Thistles
- ☐ A green sign saying 'Ribblehead Locomotive Depot'
- ☐ What number can you see on the right hand side when you walk underneath the viaduct?
- ☐ Animal feeder
- ☐ Signal box
- ☐ Train buffer

Feel

The limestone rock. Can you feel the different textures? Some of it is smooth through thousands of years of weather beating down on it, some is rougher and some parts even have lichen growing on it. Is it cold or hot? Chalk is actually a variety of limestone rock, so perhaps when you get home you could draw a picture with your own chalk!

Magnify

Limestone Rock. Limestone rock is made mostly of calcium carbonate. This comes from lots of different sources – mainly bones, teeth and shells which have formed together over millions of years to create rocks. So what you are actually looking at is just a mass of old critters!

Collect

Well, this will be a hit with the kids if nothing else – collect an ice cream at the end of the walk! There is usually an ice cream van on the opposite side of the road to the pub, a bit further down

2. When you get to another metal gate – go through it and keep straight ahead. Very shortly you will reach a junction – turn right here, following the signs for Whernside and Deepdale.

   Go through a wooden gate next to the cattle grid. You should be able to see a house to the right. Keep to this path and soon you will go over a little bridge and through another wooden gate. Keep going straight up.

   You soon have the option of either crossing a very small ford, or you could navigate around the side if you want to stay dry! This is also a good place to stop for a picnic and a paddle, weather permitting.

3. Go through the big wooden gate under the bridge, turn right and follow the path signposted 'Ribblehead'. You will go through another wooden gate or stile along this route. Eventually this will

Rebecca Terry at Ribblehead Viaduct

join up with the main path again – so rejoin the main path and keep to it with the viaduct on your right until you get back to the main road, near where you will have parked.

There is usually an ice cream van somewhere in the vicinity...

In the Area

White Scar Caves, Ingleton, LA6 3AW. Tel: 01524 241 244. Email: **info@whitescarcave.co.uk**. Let someone else do the talking for a while and enjoy this eighty minute tour around one of the natural wonders of the subterranean world. Paths and lights allow you to walk past cascading waterfalls and between massive banks of flowstone, to the massive ice-age cavern with its thousands of stalactites. There's also a café and a gift shop for those who might need jollying along... At the time of writing, it was just under twenty five pounds for a family of four.

Walk 5: Druids Temple, Ilton

Druids Temple is Yorkshire's answer to Stonehenge... It is a folly designed by a man called William Danby in 1820. The idea was to create work for the population to keep spirits up during a spell of heavy unemployment. They were paid one shilling a day. There was also an offer of a salary for someone crazy enough to live as a hermit in the temple there for seven years. I think they lasted about five... This is a good walk to do in the early autumn as there are lots of conkers to be had!

Distance	1 mile (1.7 km)
Allow	1 hour 30 minutes (including a bit of playing time at Druids Temple)
Take with you	A container to collect conkers, magnifying glass
Getting there and parking	Druids Temple is situated at the end of Knowle Lane. The best place to park is in the car park of The Bivouac, just left before the gate and down a rough track.
Map	Ordnance Survey Explorer 298
Grid Reference	177786
Post walk activity	Collecting conkers to play a game with after (see Activity 5 on page 105)

Druids Temple Checklist

Spot

- ☐ Dolmens
- ☐ Stone stack
- ☐ Bracken
- ☐ Horse chestnut tree
- ☐ Stone table and chairs
- ☐ Leighton Reservoir
- ☐ Horse barrier
- ☐ CCTV camera
- ☐ Daffodils
- ☐ Sheep
- ☐ Rabbit droppings
- ☐ A pheasant

Feel

The Druid's stones. Does all the stone feel the same? Is it the same temperature in the cave as outside on the stone seats? Put your cheek on the dolmens – do they feel different to when you touch them with your fingers?

Magnify

Pine cones. Did you know that each individual plate of the pine cone is called a scale? Can you see why? What other creature do you know about that might have scales?

Collect

Conkers. In some parts of the world, a game of conkers is called 'Kingers'. According to folk law, when you find your first conker of the season, you have to say "oddly oddly onker, my first conker" and this brings you good luck with your conker games!

To start, come out of the car park, turn right onto the rough road, so the yurts can be seen on your left behind a wall and continue until you reach Knowle lane again.

Turn left, heading up Knowle lane. You will see a (locked) gate ahead over a cattle grid. Walk round to the right of this gate and up towards the shack car park.

At the top of the car park, you will see a signpost for 'Public footpath, Druids Temple Only'. Follow this sign to the right. It's a grassy track with newly planted trees at either side.

After about 150 metres, veer right off this tree-lined track, heading downwards (you should see a black barn almost ahead in the distance). Cleared woodland is either side of you, with more mature wood to the far left. Follow this path down towards the bottom of the wood, where you will see an open, wooden gate.

Dolmen at Druids Temple, Ilton

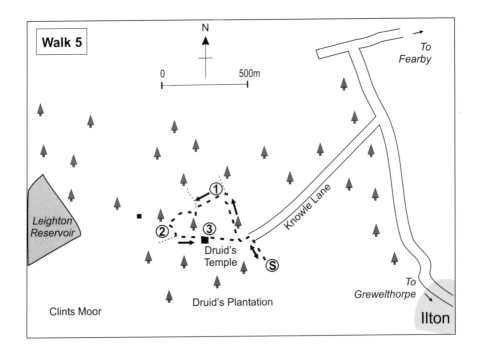

Keep straight ahead (ignoring a small left turn) until you almost reach another gate.

1. Turn left before the gate and follow the path round with the wall on your right and wood on the left. You should be able to see Fearby church on your right in the distance.

   The path becomes denser and eventually you will spot the reservoir in the distance. Take the left turn, uphill, heading away from the stile in the wall. Then, in about fifteen metres, turn right, following the path back towards the wall.

2. After a few minutes, take the left path uphill, heading away from the gate and the reservoir in the distance (NB if you reach the stone barn, you have gone too far).

   A dolmen will come into view at the top of this hill. Here, is looks a bit like a grassy roundabout. Walk straight on ahead, past the dolmen and in about two hundred metres, the folly will come into view. This is a great place to let the kids play/have a picnic.

3. When you are ready to leave, just re-join the path, heading in the same direction. This will lead you back to the shack car park within about five minutes. Go through the car park and head down Knowle lane. Turn right when you reach High Knowle Farm and continue downhill until you see the Bivouac Reception car park on your left. And you're back!

This is a great place to eat/drink and there's even a family room full of toys for the children.

In the Area
At the time of writing, Bivouac were planning on running forest schools for children – where they learn to build dens, learn about the forest etc... But please ring to check times and prices on 01765 53 50 20 before you set off for the day.

Or why not have a bash at pony trekking? Masham Riding and Trekking Centre, Dykes Hill House, Masham, HG4 4NS. **www.mashamridingcentre.com**. Tel: 01756 689 636 or 01756 689241. You don't have to go for long – the shortest trek is fifteen minutes – or you could stretch it to two hours, depending on how you feel. There are nine trekking routes within the Swinton Estate, which cover approximately twenty two thousand acres of The Yorkshire Dales. The treks are always supervised by an experienced member of staff. There is a minimum age of seven – and you must book in advance on one of the numbers above. Cost-wise, at the time of writing, a fifteen minute trek started at eight pounds per person – but there may be group deals to be had.

Walk 6: Stainforth (Catrigg Force)

This is a great walk with lovely views, taking in Catrigg Force waterfall along the way. Catrigg force plunges six metres over a single drop into a narrow rocky gorge – and is even listed as one of The Yorkshire Dales top thirty waterfalls! This walk is pretty steep in the first leg, but once you are at the top it is plain sailing. As well as the beautiful countryside, it is also worth noting that the Stainforth Environmental Group has put a lot of effort into their Road Verges Project – in a bid enhance the quality of wildlife on the roadside verges. So look out for the lovely lilacs

Distance	2.25 miles (3.6 km)
Allow	1 hour 45 minutes (more if you are having a picnic and playing near the waterfall
Take with you	Magnifying glass, small towel to dry hands after choosing a stone from the stream
Getting there and parking	Stainforth is situated just off the B6479 north of Settle. Park in the tourist car park (don't forget to pay and display)
Map	Ordnance Survey Explorer OL2
Grid Reference	820672
Post walk activity	Stone painting. Collect a stone from the stream at the end of the walk, and take home to paint (see Activity 6 on page 106)

and purples of chicory and vetch - or you might even see some yellow
birds foot trefoil or some yarrow along the way.

Leave the car park turning right onto the road. Stay on this pavement.
It soon veers round to the right.

1. Pass over a stone bridge and should see the Craven Heifer pub on
   your right. Cross the road here and follow the path which says
   'PBW'. Very shortly you get to another little junction and there is
   Croft House in front. Turn right and then immediately left,
   following the footpath for Winskill (it's up a rubble track, passing
   some lovely cottages on the left).

   Very soon you will arrive at a wooden gate - go through the gate
   and follow the grassy path straight ahead. Soon you will see
   another open gate at the top left - go through that one and then
   keep to the little rubble path heading upwards.

2. In this field you will see a small wooden post stuck out of the
   ground, painted yellow. This is leading the way to the footpath - it's
   open fields really. There are a few of these which lead you to the
   wire fencing, rather than the stone wall.
   You will see another wooden post with a public footpath sign - just
   keep to this, still heading upwards on the small track. When you
   see a kissing gate on the left, go through this and up the very rocky
   steps (it's pretty steep).

   When you reach the top there is a ladder stile. Go over this and
   stick to the trodden path over the fields. Eventually you will come
   to another ladder stile with a gate at the side. Unfortunately you
   have to take the stile as the gate does not open! Follow the footpath
   sign, heading away from the main road now and we are almost at
   the top of the hill.

3. A farm will come into view on the left. Don't follow the path down
   to another ladder stile. Instead, keep straight on where you will
   soon see a metal gate (just around the corner on the left). When
   you are through (or over) that gate, head towards the middle of the
   farm, go through it and turn right following the public footpath
   sign with walls at either side of a dirt track.

Stainforth Checklist

Spot

- ☐ Sheep
- ☐ Limestone rock
- ☐ Static caravans (in the distance)
- ☐ Cows
- ☐ Ladder stile
- ☐ Farm
- ☐ Winskill stone
- ☐ Quarry
- ☐ Waterfall (Catrigg Force)
- ☐ Geese
- ☐ Chickens
- ☐ Stepping stones
- ☐ Church clock

Feel

Sheeps wool. There should be some on the ground through the fields, or bits on barbed wire. How does it feel? Soft and fluffy? Waxy? Can you imagine a jumper being made out of this?

Magnify

Winskill stones. These are the rocky stones found in the fields you are walking through. They are made of carboniferous limestone, hence their pale/chalky appearance. What can you see up close? Are they all the same colour? Do they look bumpy?

Collect

Stone from the stream near the end of the walk – to paint when you return home

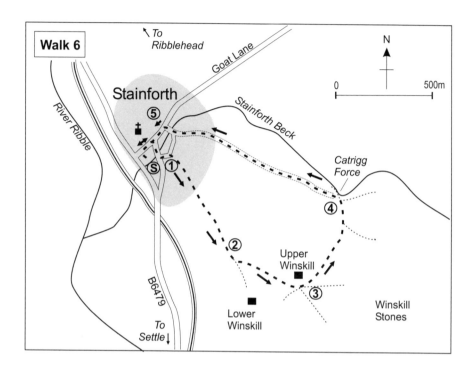

You will reach a cattle grid with a gate at the side. Go through the gate and follow the signpost up ahead to 'Pennine Bridleway, Stainforth 1¾ miles'. It seems a bit confusing here, as the signpost looks like you should go straight over the wall – but don't. Just head towards the wall and then just keep the wall to your left and carry on.

This track takes you through an open wooden gate – just keep straight to this. (NB: the stones that you will see on the ground are Winskill stones and on the left in the distance you should see some quarry works). Eventually you will come to another basic track right in front of this one (almost like a junction). Join this new track heading down left through a gateway, again just following the signs for 'Pennine Bridleway, Stainforth'.

4. When you reach a wooden gate, go through it and then you can either: keep going straight on or head right through another gate

signed to 'Catrigg Force' to see the waterfall. If you do go to see the waterfall (which we recommend), simply just make your way back up to this point when you are ready to continue the walk.

So continuing on then... Follow this track down. It eventually turns into a more structured tarmac path where you will see some houses either side (and if you are lucky some geese and chickens on your left in a field). When you come to the central grass area in the middle, keep to the right, passing Green End Cottage on your right. Then cross over some stepping stones (a good place to find a rock to paint when you get home), follow the path round past a house on your left (Wynders House), rejoin the road and head down left.

5. When you get to the junction, cross the road and get onto the 'pavement, heading right and following signs for Horton in Ribblesdale 3½ miles'. This takes you straight back to the car park.

Two asleep, two with tired legs and one munching his teeshirt

In the Area

You could mosey into the village of Stainforth, or just a mile away is the market town of Settle with plenty of cafés and shops to peruse.

Or if you're not in a rush, about five and a half miles out of Stainforth is The Falconry Centre, Crows nest road, nr Giggleswick, North Yorkshire, LA2 8AS. Tel: 01729 822 832. **www.hawkexperience.com**. Set in dramatic limestone surroundings, the Falconry Centre's main aim is to educate – highlighting the fact that many of the world's birds of prey are under threat of extinction. There are around thirty five birds of prey at The Falconry Centre – including various species of vultures, hawks, falcons and owls from around the world. Please check the website or call first so you can time your trip to co-incide with one of the displays. There is also a tearoom and children's adventure playground. At the time of writing, a family ticket (two adults and two children) was twenty one pounds.

Walk 7: Settle

Settle is one of the most scenic towns in the Yorkshire Dales - and the starting point for the famous Settle-Carlisle Railway. The town stands beside the largest outcrop of limestone in Britain – with cliffs, caves, scars and potholes in abundance. If you are not bound by weekends and like a good market stall, do this walk on a Tuesday to enjoy Settle

Distance	3.2 miles (5.1 km)
Allow	2 hours for the walk – longer if you stay in Settle afterwards
Take with you	Bread for ducks, magnifying glass, something to keep your pine cone in
Getting there and parking	Drive into Settle on the B6480 and park in the car park opposite The Fishermans Fish Restaurant and near the Co-operative and BP garage
Map	Ordnance Survey Explorer OL2
Grid Reference	819638
Post walk activity	Pine Cone bird feeder. This is a quick (but messy) activity to do after the walk. Don't forget to collect your pine cone along the way (see Activity 7 on page 108)

On Route in Settle

Market at its best – lots of produce either locally sourced or handmade. We suggest doing the walk in the morning, then having lunch in one of the many cafés in or around the area. Our route takes you out of the town centre, along the River Ribble, over bridges, through fields, past a reservoir and back into the Settle - just enough for you to build up an appetite or thirst!

Walk out of the car park, turn right and cross the main road, heading towards the church, then head straight on underneath the bridge. Stay on this pavement for quite a while.

1. Soon you will reach a road, with signposts for Giggleswick and Kendal. Cross straight over this road and keep going – heading over the bridge over the River Ribble. Then turn right following a signpost marked Public Footpath, Ribble Way, Stackhouse ¾ mile. There is a wooden fence on the left.

Settle Checklist

Spot

- ☐ Rugby goal posts
- ☐ Mill chimneys
- ☐ Sheep
- ☐ Big green barn door
- ☐ Horse jump
- ☐ Tractor
- ☐ Manhole cover
- ☐ What type of bird is on the Lock Cottage sign?
- ☐ Ducks
- ☐ Sluice gate
- ☐ Railway bridge
- ☐ Wheel on the side of the mill

Feel

Horse chesnut tree trunk. Are there rough ridges or smooth lines? Does it feel the same using your fingertips as it does if you used the back of your hand? I'll bet you can't reach one of the branches...

Magnify

A cow pat! But hold your nose – it might be a bit stinky... What does it look like? What colour is it? Can you see any dung beetles on it? Did you know that in some places in India, cow pat is dried out in the sun and used for fuel?

Collect

Pine cone

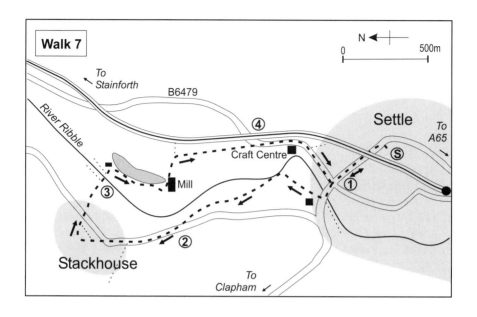

Keep to this path and follow it round so the River Ribble will eventually be flowing downwards on your right. After a while the path turns left, away from the river (you should still have the school playing fields on your left). This eventually comes to a brick wall end. So from here, go over the gap stile on the right hand side and through the field, following the trodden path straight across to the other side and over another stile. Once over the stile, keep to the path with the wall on your left.

2. When the wall runs out, just keep going straight ahead anyway. You will go through two stiles after this, then through the field, then a small gate which takes you onto a little road, where you will turn right towards Stackhouse.

After a while you will cross a road and see a Public Bridleway sign to Stackhouse, which you need to follow, round to the right. You will pass Carrholme House. The path eventually opens up again, so turn right and very shortly it comes to a little road again. So, turn left and then almost immediate right where it says 'Public Footpath

Ribble Way, Stainforth 1¼ miles', past Ribble Land house and through a little wooden gate.

3. This path will bring you out at the weir. Turn right here and cross over the river. Then turn right again and go down through two rows of terrace houses. Then at Lock Cottage, turn left following the 'Public Footpath' sign.

   Go through the wooden gate and you will see a small reservoir straight ahead. Turn right (with the reservoir on your right). Keep to this path and go over a little stone bridge, then follow this path until you reach some buildings. Follow this path round to the left (with the reservoir and sluice gate on your left). You will pass a mill on your right as the path slopes gently downwards. Go down the steps and turn left onto a pavement (you should see a 'No Entry' sign right up ahead of you in the distance).

4. This leads to a junction, where you need to turn right. This road takes you to another junction of a main road. Cross over the road onto the pavement at the other side and keep going in the same direction towards the Mill chimney (you should pass Watershed Mill Craft Centre on your right).

   At the end of this road is a junction (you should see a house just to the right over the road which has lots of chimneys). Turn left at this junction, keeping to the pavement. Go under the bridge again and you will see the garage and car park on your right.

In the Area

If you want to really want to expand your day – why not hop on the Settle-Carlisle railway? It runs through some of the most attractive scenery in the Yorkshire Dales and Cumbrian Fells.

A popular place to stop off is Appleby – particularly during Appleby Horse Fair, which is an annual gathering of travellers, usually the first week in June – from Thursday to the following Wednesday. It's a lively atmosphere with plenty to see including horses being washed in the river, raced down the streets and lots of stalls. It is not an organised event, so there is no entrance fee and no need to book. For the train ticket though, you can either buy it at the station, online at **www.settle-carlisle.co.uk** or by calling the Freephone number 0800 980 0766.

Or if you're feeling energetic, there's a public swimming pool in nearby Giggleswick – but ring first for opening times: 01729 823 626 or check the website **www.settleswimmingpool.co.uk**

Walk 8 : Malham Cove

Malham is probably one of the most popular villages in the Yorkshire Dales - though it never seems too busy. It is host to Malham Cove - a huge crag (eighty metres high/three hundred metres wide) which has been the nesting place for a pair of peregrine falcons since 1993. The emerging stream from the crag flows right through the village. The limestone paths are typical of this area of The Yorkshire Dales. About fifteen thousand years ago, this area was covered with ice sheets and glaciers. The ice swept down from the north, scouring the landscape - and one of the most distinctive features of this glaciation is the formation of the limestone pavements.

Distance	2.3 miles (3.7 km)
Allow	1 hour 30 minutes (more if stopping for picnic)
Take with you	A towel for the children as the stream is very tempting in hot weather, bag for a few daisies, magnifying glass
Getting there and parking	Take the road signposted for Malham from the A65 at Gargrave. Park in the National Park Centre (it is a Pay & Display)
Map	Ordnance Survey Explorer OL2
Grid Reference	900627
Post walk activity	Making Dinosaur footprint (see Activity 8 on page 109

This circular route offers a real mix of terrain and scenery, whatever the weather. If it's looking like the rain will hold off, take a picnic for a perfect half-way stop in front of the spectacular cove. For those who don't fancy carting a picnic around, you won't be disappointed with the local cafés or pubs. Sometimes the village hall is open for home-made sandwiches and cakes made by the Women's Institute.

Walk out of the car park heading towards the main road. Cross the road towards the stream and with the stream on your right walk up towards the village. You will soon see The Buck Inn on your left. Cross over the road here and keep heading up. You will pass some public toilets on your left and some cottages on either side.

1. Shortly you will see a red telephone box on the other side of the street. Cross the road and head towards it. There is a little wooden gate on the left which leads to a wooded area. Go through this gate and follow the path with the stream to your right. It is in this

Malham Cove

Malham Checklist

Spot

- ☐ Red telephone box
- ☐ Dinosaur footprint
- ☐ Milk churn
- ☐ Peregrine falcon
- ☐ Wrought iron kingfisher bird
- ☐ Barny the owl
- ☐ Animal feeder
- ☐ Stone bench

Feel

If it is warm enough, take your shoes and socks off and dip your toes into the water near the cove. Can you describe what the water feels like? What else can you feel under your feet? Stones? Weeds? Moss? When you take your foot out of the water, does it feel hotter or colder than when it is in the water?

Magnify

Feather. Can you see how it is hard in the middle, like a spine and then softer around the edges? Does it tickle if you brush it under your nose? Birds need feathers for a variety of reasons; obviously to help them fly, to keep them warm, for camouflage and also to let other birds know if they are male or female. The longest feather ever recorded came from an ornamental chicken bred in Japan – its tail feather measured 10.59m or 34.75ft long.

Collect

Daisies – to make a daisy chain along the way

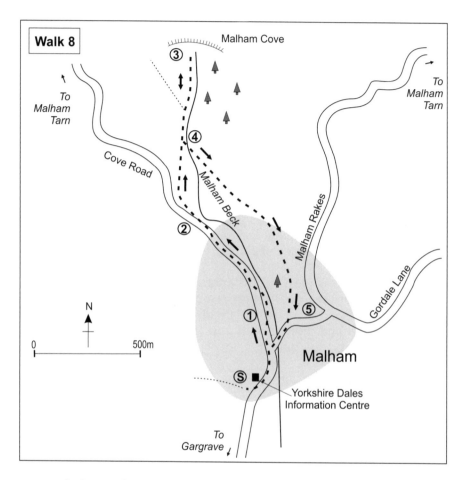

wooded area that you should see some dinosaur footprints... When you get to the wooden gate at the other end, go through and turn right onto the road.

You will pass Beck Hall and Town Head Barn on the right. It is worth popping into the barn as it has some interesting facts about agriculture in Malham through the ages. Barny the Owl is also to be found in here...

2. Past the barn you will get to a wooden footpath gate. Go through it and follow the path left. (If the weather is nice, you will probably

spot a few tents around here as there is a campsite). You will go through a few wooden gates along this path and then eventually it comes to a kind of fork, which takes you either up to the top or right towards the cove. Take the path towards the cove with the stream on your right. This is a lovely place to stop for a picnic or simply admire the view. If the weather is good, it's also a great paddling spot.

3. After you have had a rest here, turnaround and head back in the direction you came, passing through one wooden gate.

4. You will soon see and ancient stone bridge over the stream on your left (a clapper bridge). Cross over the bridge and go through the wooden gate at the other side. Then head up and right as if you are going up round the edge of the hill and onto a stony path.

   At the top of this path you will come to a grassy meadow – just keep going until you go through a wooden gate. You may see a sign which says 'Bomby's Barn – Malham Tarn Estate'. Head through another field and another gate too. This eventually leads onto a more structured footpath.

   Go through a kissing gate and just keep to this path, going through any gates you come across. At one point there will be walls either side of you.

5. Eventually you will pass Malham Youth Hostel on your left and, not long after, will come to a junction with the Worcester Arms pub on the right. Turn right here and go over the bridge, where you will see The Buck Inn pub again. Turn left over the bridge and into a wooden gate and head downstream until you get to another wooden gate at the other side. Go though the gate, pass the Old Barn Café on your right, cross the road and turn right back into the car park.

In the Area

You may also wish to tie your walk in with 'The Malham Safari' or duck race. These usually take place in June half term. Buy a safari sheet for a couple of pounds from most shops/cafés in the area (correct at time of writing) and stroll around the village to find the answers to the clues. For more information go to **www.malhamdale.com**.

Or, on August Bank Holiday Saturday, Malham Show is well worth a visit (see same website). It's a traditional agricultural and family country show, which has been going on for over a hundred years. It has the usual showjumping, farmers markets, falconry displays, stalls, handicrafts and childrens rides etc.. It's usually around twelve pounds for a family ticket.

Walk 9: Grassington

Grassington is so beautiful that some of the residents claim it's twinned with Paradise! Enjoy a whole day here – with this easy but lovely walk in the morning and a saunter around the historic village in the afternoon (host to some great family owned shops, pubs and cosy cafés). The walk is based around the River Wharfe, taking in a

Distance	2.2 miles (3.5 km)
Allow	1 hour 30 minutes
Take with you	Towel for drying feet after paddling, some paper and crayons, bread for the ducks, bag for collectables
Getting there and parking	Park in the main National Centre car park. We recommend giving yourself three hours on a ticket, which should include enough time for a nosey round the village. At the time of writing this, costs were about £3.20 per vehicle
Map	Ordnance Survey Explorer OL2
Grid Reference	002637
Post walk activity	Making a Yorkshire Rose flag with the rubbings from the walk (see Activity 9 on page 111)

sixteenth century church along the way. There is plenty of space for a picnic and you may even be able to buy a pair of socks from outside one of the houses you will pass!

From the car park, turn to face downhill into the overspill car park. You will see a wooden gate at the bottom left-hand corner. Go through the gate and turn right, to head down quite a narrow path.

1. At the bottom of the path you will come to a wooden bridge over the river Wharfe. Cross over the bridge and follow the path round to the right until you come to a T-junction (there is a stone bridge to the right).

2. Turn left at this T-junction with a high wall to your left and then veer right to join the road. Turn left along this road (passing Falls House, built in 1890) and just keep straight on until you arrive at the Saint Michael and All Angels church. (It is along this path where

A lovely spot for a picnic in Grassington

Grassington Checklist

Spot

- ☐ 'Welcome to Grassington' sign
- ☐ Stone bridge
- ☐ A Spring
- ☐ Bird House
- ☐ Sign with AD 1631
- ☐ Sluice Gate
- ☐ Angel Gargoyle
- ☐ An anchor (on a gravestone)

Feel

Close your eyes and, with your fingers, feel the different letters from the engravings on the benches in the church yard. Can you tell which letters they are without peeping?

Magnify

Stop on the grass near the river (good place for a picnic). Over one small section of ground, count how many different tiny things you can see. Can you see any small bugs? Can you see the mud underneath the grass? Are there any droplets of water on the grass (dew). Imagine how many blades of grass there must be if there are so many under just one magnifying glass...

Collect

A good stick for the pole of your Yorkshire Rose flag

you might see socks for sale outside somebody's house!). You will also pass some public toilets along this way.

This is the church where you can do some rubbings (see Activity 18 on page 127). Can you find a Yorkshire rose on one of the benches? It is also worth mentioning that, at the time of writing, inside the church were some leaflets on trails to do with children (40p). They were aimed at slightly older that this book, but may be worth picking up for future reference...

3. After you have walked around the church grounds, turn back the way you came and head towards Falls House again.

   At Falls House turn right (so you will pass the high wall on your right) and you will come to a stone footbridge. Cross over the bridge and keep to the beaten grass path with the river on your right and a small row of houses on your left. Soon you will see a

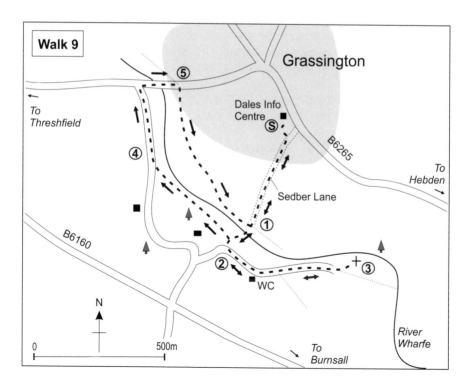

little stone beach area which would be a nice place to stop for a juice or to throw some stones into the river.

In no time at all you will see a wooden gate towards to the left. Go through this gate and keep to the narrow path (single file!), passing the old mill on your right.

4. Eventually you will reach another wooden gate. Go through the gate and turn right onto the road. There is no pavement here, so take extra care. Keep going until you get to a main junction. Cross over the road to the side with a pavement and turn right, crossing over the bridge (following the signs to 'Grassington (½ mile)'.

5. Just after you pass the 'Welcome to Grassington' sign, you will be able to cross the road again, to go through a wooden gate, then another wooden gate, to take you back down towards the river (it should then be on your right). This is a lovely place for a picnic.

Keep to this path all the way until you reach another wooden gate (where you will see the first wooden bridge you crossed near the beginning of the walk). Go through the gate and turn left for a last burst of energy up the steep hill again.

At the top of the hill you will spot the wooden gate on your left which leads you back into the car park.

To visit the village of Grassington, head to the top of the car park to the main road, turn left and you will be at the shops/pubs/cafés in five minutes.

In The Area

Right in the town centre of Grassington is Upper Wharfedale Folk Museum, The Square, Grassington, BD23 5AQ. This is one to do after the walk as it's only open between 1400-1630 – and from Tuesday to Sunday. The museum provides reminders of yesteryear including exhibits of lead mining, craft tools, dales farming, period costume and folklore. Check ahead for entry prices (if any) on: 01756 753287. It is a registered charity and at the time of writing, no prices were available.

Or, if you want to time your walk with The Grassington Festival, it's usually held in June and offers theatre, music, comedy, film and visual arts. Some events are free. Check ahead as dates and attractions may vary. **www.grassington-festival.org.uk** or ring: 01756 752 691.

Walk 10: Pateley Bridge

Pately Bridge is situated right in the heart of a special landscape designated as an Area of Outstanding Natural Beauty. It is part of a Six hundred and three square kilometre section of land which extends from Ellingstring to Otley and Fountains Abbey to Middlesmoor. This walk takes in some of the more gentle farming landscapes, which still provide important habitats for many creatures large and small. The

Distance	1.9 miles (3.1 km)
Allow	1 hour 15 minutes
Take with you	Something to collect your blackberries in, magnifying glass, towel for drying hands
Getting there and parking	Take the road to Lofthouse and Gouthwaite Reservoir from Pateley Bridge. Park off Low Wath Road at The Bridge Inn pub car park (on the left as you enter the car park)
Map	Ordnance Survey Explorer 298
Grid Reference	148663
Post walk activity	Make krispie bird nest when you get home (see Actity 10 on page 112)

Waterwheel visible from pub car park at the beginning of the walk

walk begins near a pub car park away from the village centre - a perfect excuse to work up a thirst along the way... To make a day out of this walk, combine it with a visit to the village centre - there are plenty of little shops and cafés as well as some lovely spots along the River Nidd to enjoy a picnic or fish and chips.

To start the walk, exit the pub car park and turn left, heading over the bridge. Shortly after you have crossed the bridge, turn left, following a sign which says 'Heathfield ¾ mile'.

1. After another short while, turn left again following a sign to 'Westfield and Low Wood Caravan Site & Heathfield Caravan Park'. You end up actually walking through the caravan site.

2. Go over a cattle grid and head straight on. When you reach a metal gate on the left hand side (next to a sign for 'Low Wood Caravan

Pateley Bridge Checklist

Spot

- ☐ Water wheel
- ☐ Caravan
- ☐ Tractor
- ☐ Hazelnut tree
- ☐ Sheep droppings
- ☐ Stream
- ☐ The date Heathfield caravan park was made – (1855)
- ☐ Blackberry bushes
- ☐ A bridge
- ☐ Moss/lichen on a dry stone wall

Feel

Holding your childs' other hand, get him or her to roll up their sleeve and put their hand in the stream. When does the current feel the strongest – when your fingers are spread wide open or when they are closed together?

Magnify

Sheep droppings. But do not touch them, and give your hands a wipe after. Also, do not try this activity during lambing season as it may frighten them. What do the droppings look like up close? They usually start off as something called 'crotties' which are solid masses, but easily split to look like pellets. Sheep like eating mainly grass and hay, but in the run up to lambing time, farmers often give them barley and nuts for extra nutrition

Collect

Backberries to make blackberry pie at home

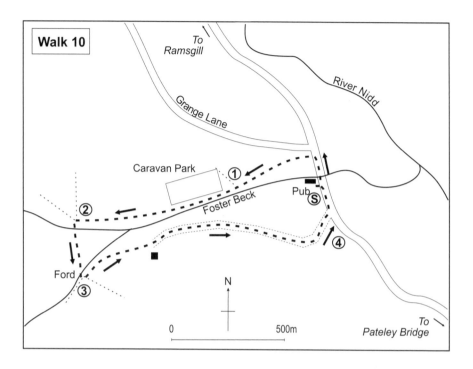

Site'), go through the gate, straight on, over a bridge and through a black gate to follow a stony path upwards.

3. At the top of this little path, follow it round, veering left between two walls. Eventually you will come to a tiny little footbridge (which is not suitable for a pram). So either cross over the footbridge or go through the ford. This would be a nice place to stop and throw a few stones in the water or have a paddle.

   Once you have crossed the water, head up then turn left, going through a red gate. (You will pass the house on your left). Go through another red gate then just stick to this path. It will take you through fields and over a cattle grid.

4. Eventually this path ends by joining the road. Turn left onto the road and follow it back to the Bridge Inn pub.

In The Area

There's a great childrens play park in Grassington, which is free. In the summertime it can get pretty busy as it's often used by the nearby camping/caravan sites.

Nidderdale Museum, King Street, HG3 5LE is right in the centre of Pately Bridge; it's a collection of exhibits displayed in the original Victorian workhouse, illustrating the life and history of Dalesfolk. At the time of writing it cost under a fiver for a family of four. For more details go to **www.nidderdalemuseum.com** or call: 01423 711 225.

Or... if you fancied combining this walk with Nidderdade Agricultural Show, held in nearby Brewerley Park, do it in September. It has everything you would expect to see at a Yorkshire Agricultural Show – livestock and horses, craft tents, sheep dog trials... for specific dates and details go to **www.nidderdaleshow.co.uk** or ring: 01969 650 129.

Walk 11: Ripley Castle Perimeter

       £

In 2009 the Inglebys celebrated seven hundred years of their family living at Ripley Castle. This walk takes you around the perimeter of that Castle – allowing for at-a-distance views of how the other half live(d). You will also be able to see fallow deer meandering around in the acres of land as well as some not-so-glamorous pigs on the way back! Crossing fields and streams, yet with decent paths, this is a lovely walk to do in most weathers.

Distance	2.9 miles (4.6 km)
Allow	2 hours
Take with you	Paper and crayons to do some rubbings, magnifying glass, bag for collectables
Getting there and parking	Ripley is situated on the A61 between Harrogate and Ripon. Park in the main Ripley village car park
Map	Ordnance Survey Explorer 298
Grid Reference	284603
Post walk activity	Make-your-own-castle (see Activity 11 on page 114). You could also decorate the castle walls with some of the rubbings you might have done on this walk (see Activity 18 on page 127)

Ripley Castle Perimeter Checklist

Spot

☐ A cross
☐ Teddy bears on a sign
☐ A stone boar. When did Ripley receive the stone boar gift?
(Ans: 1907)
☐ Union Flag
☐ Turrets
☐ Coat of Arms
☐ Deer
☐ When was Park Lodge built? (Ans: 1848)

Feel

A fallen tree with coins in. What different textures can you feel?
Notice how the edges of the coins feel smooth, but the rest of the
tree is rough. Is it wet or dry? Are the coins a different temperature
to the rest of the wood?

Magnify

As above (fallen tree with coins), but look more closely. What sort
of coins can you see? How many different denominations are
there? Can you see any dates on them? Which is the oldest coin?
What does the bark look like up close? Are there any creatures
crawling about in it?

Collect

A good place to do some rubbings is at the church which you pass
on the way to the castle. You could then cut these out and use
them as decorations for the inside of your castle, when you return
home

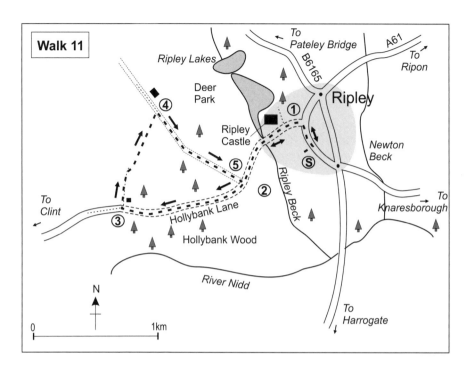

Head out of the car park through the kissing gate following the signs for Hotel De Ville, Nidderdale Way, Market Square etc...towards the Boars Head pub.

1. Turn left just before the pub towards the castle. You will pass the church on your left. If you have brought a crayon and some paper, this would be a good place to do a few rubbings (see Activity 18 on page 127) . You will also pass the castle on your right.

   You will soon see a wooden gate. There is a lot of space either side of it, so just make your way through. This is called Hollybank Lane (which is part of the Roman road from Ilkley). After a short while, cross over a stone bridge over a lovely waterfall. This would be a good place for pooh sticks (see Activity 16 on page 124). You should be able to see the deer park in the distance to your right while standing on this bridge. So once you have crossed the bridge, just keep to the uphill path.

2. Very shortly, this path forks. Take the smaller, left hand path through the trees. Eventually this small path just rejoins the larger one. When it does, just keep to it, through an open wooden gate and you will see anther fork. Take the left hand public bridleway to 'Hollybank Lodge, Clint and Hampsthwaite'.

3. After quite a while, this path reaches a big wooden gate and a smaller gate to the left. Walk through the smaller gate, turn right and head in between the house and a fence following signs for the public footpath.

4. Soon you will arrive at a wooden kissing gate, go through this and keep straight ahead. This path gets greener and wider, so just keep to the edge. Eventually you will arrive at another kissing gate. Go through the gate which meets a more structured road and turn right. You will pass a lovely house called Park Lodge on the left and some old farm building on the right.

View of the back of Ripley Castle from the perimeter path

5. This road eventually forks, leading back to the signpost for 'Clint and Hampsthwaite'. So turn left, follow the sign for 'Ripley' which will take you back over the bridge and up the hill, all the way back to the castle. At this point you can either visit the courtyard and castle on the left or keep to the pavement, following it past the church, and then veer round to the car park again.

In the Area

There are various seasonal events which you may want to tie in with this walk – such as Ripley Show, Classic Car rallies and Christmas Festivals.

Or why not simply take a tour around the castle and gardens while you're there? Ripley's colourful and gruesome history is perfect for those little ones with an active imagination; then there's the walled garden, kitchen garden and a lovely Lakeland path. Check before you go for prices and specific events at **www.ripleycastle.co.uk** or by phoning: 01423 770 152.

Walk 12: Skipton Woods

Skipton Woods is a real treat in the heart of this Yorkshire town. As well as beautiful woodland, featuring amazing wildlife (woodpeckers, kingfishers and even heron) this circular walk also manages to incorporate the sight of the medieval Skipton Castle. If it's the right season you will also see carpets of bluebells and wild garlic. The pond in the middle is perfect for a pond-dipping activity (please take a small plastic container for this; see page 125 for pond dipping instructions). The market town of Skipton is bustling and there are lots of places to eat and drink – from vegetarian cafés to pub carveries.

Distance	2.3 miles (3.7 km)
Allow	1 hour 30 minutes
Take with you	Plastic container for scooping out some pond water, magnifying glass, wipes, bag for collectables
Getting there and parking	Park in the Canal side car park, which is near to the Tourist Information Centre. It's worth noting that there are toilets here before you set off
Map	Ordnance Survey Explorer OL2
Grid Reference	987517
Post walk activity	Make a clock face. This links in with spotting the church clock on the walk (see Activity 12 on page 116)

Sam and Emma figure out the sluice gate in Skipton Woods

The walk starts from the main entrance of the car park. Turn left here, so the Tourist Information Centre in on your left. Cross over the road and join the canal path, walking away from the car park with the canal on your right. Soon you will be able to see the castle wall high up on your right (and hopefully the Union flag)

1. Eventually, this path comes to a halt (quite literally a brick wall in front). Turn left here, heading over a little bridge and up some steps, then follow the path to the right (which then veers left). You will come to an opening with a sign which says 'Permissive Footpath, through Private Road'. Turn right here and head through the smallholding towards a large gate. One of these houses used to be the old sawmill. You will also see a 'Skipton Woods' sign.

   Go through the metal gate and over the footbridge, heading upwards toward the 'Skipton Woods' sign. Now, just keep to this path.

Skipton Woods Checklist

Spot

- ☐ Canal boats
- ☐ Wild garlic
- ☐ Woodpecker
- ☐ Ducks
- ☐ Waterwheel
- ☐ Union Flag
- ☐ Waterfall
- ☐ Leeds/Liverpool Heritage Trail stumps
- ☐ Sluice gate (next to pond)
- ☐ Holly
- ☐ Church clock
- ☐ Weather vane

Feel

Wild garlic. Reach down into the beds of wild garlic and run your hands through it. What does it feel like? Does it tickle? And what does it smell like? Does it smell similar to anything else you know?

Magnify

Some pond water. Scoop some water into a plastic container and see what you can see. (Don't forget to give your hands a wipe after this activity as pond water contains many germs). Is anything moving in the water? Can you see any tiny plankton? It is clear or muddy? What does it smell like? Does it look the same colour in your container compared to the whole of the rest of the pond?

Collect

Feathers. Look closely on the ground. You could probably find a duck feather near the pond and maybe one from another type of bird elsewhere. This is a tricky one – but you never know!

2. Eventually you will come to another metal bridge – cross over it. Straight ahead is a lake/pond (where, at the time of writing, there were two nesting herons – so you might just be lucky and spot them). This is also where you could do a bit of pond dipping (see page 125) for the 'magnify' section of this walk – or a good spot for a picnic as there are a couple of benches here too. Anyway, to continue...follow the obvious path round to the left (with the pond on your right).

Soon there is a smaller path off to the right, but just ignore it and keep straight ahead. Around here could be a good spot to throw some stones into the water or collect some duck feathers.

3. You will eventually come to the end of the path, where you can see two tunnels over the beck to your left. Turn right, heading up some steps and follow the path round to the right.

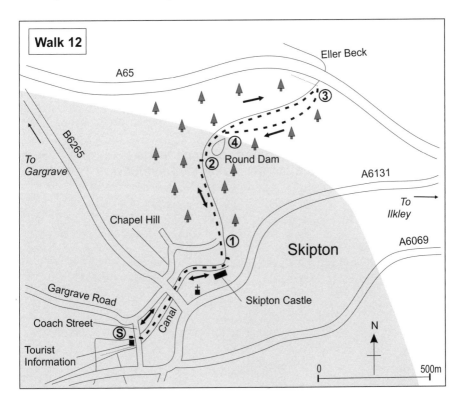

After a while, the path veers left over a little bridge. After you have crossed the bridge, turn sharp right and head down some steps. At the bottom of the steps, follow the path down to the left which brings you out at the pond.

4. With the pond on your left, keep to this route, then cross over the bridge on your right again and just retrace your steps to the car park.

In The Area

Skipton Castle is over nine hundred years old, yet is one of the most complete and well-preserved of castles in England. You can wander round most rooms in the castle from right at the top in the watchtower, to the lowest depths of the dungeons. Check for opening times and prices before you set off **www.skiptoncastle.co.uk** or call: 01756 792 442. At the time of writing, a family of four could get in for just over twenty pounds.

Or, if you'd rather rest your legs, hop on a canal boat tour down the Leeds Liverpool canal. There are thirty minute and sixty minute trips available – departing from Coach Street, BD23 1LH. This is the number if you want to book ahead: 01756 790 829, or visit their website at **www.canaltrips.co.uk**.

Or... if you want to mooch round the open markets in town, they're open Mon, Wed, Fri and Sat (including Bank holidays) – from 0900-1700.

Walk 13: Bolton Abbey

This is a great historic walk with something for everyone. You will see The Priory ruins, which date back to the 12th Century (the church is still open) and the views along the river Wharfe are amazing in all seasons. This takes you over water, through open fields, along paths and through the woods. Ash and silver birch trees are popular around here

Distance	2.1 miles (3.4 km)
Allow	1 hour 30 minutes
Take with you	Bread for the ducks, a few coins to stick into a fallen tree along the way, small towel for after paddling
Getting there and parking	Go to www.boltonabbey.com and follow the link. For satnavs, the postcode is BD23 6EX. For map readers, you want the B6160. Park in the car park at Cavendish Pavillion (low season free, high season about five pounds per vehicle at time of writing)
Map	Ordnance Survey Explorer OL2
Grid Reference	078551
Post walk activity	Make a St Georges Cross flag – you should spot one on the walk near the abbey (see Activity 13 on page 118)

Bolton Abbey Checklist

Spot

- ☐ Ducks
- ☐ Lifebouy
- ☐ Triangular warning sign
- ☐ Flag of St Georges Cross
- ☐ Sheep
- ☐ Stepping stones
- ☐ Waterfall from a pipe
- ☐ Priory
- ☐ Gargoyles

Feel

Sand on the beach. Does it run through your fingers or is it wet and hard? Did you know that sand is actually made from rocks and stones and minerals and bones which have slowly been ground down through the weather and time into tiny particles?

Magnify

Duck poo. Don't touch it though. Is it just one colour or a mixture of colours? Does it look solid or runny? What does it smell like? Did you know that ducks can poo both in and out of water?

Collect

Some duck feathers. Try to find at least three – of varying sizes and colours.

*and if you're lucky, you may even spot a money tree! There's a great café to re-charge your batteries at the end of this walk; and if you're taking the family dog, an outside tap and a couple of bowls sit outside to quench their thirst too. There are often seasonal events at Bolton Abbey, like Easter Egg hunts, crafts in the summer holidays etc, so have a nosey at the website if you want to tie the walk in with one of these (**www.boltonabbey.com**) or call 01756 718 000.*

Head towards the café, with the river on your right.

1. Turn right and to go over the bridge. At the end of the bridge, go right again through a wooden gate, taking you along a public footpath toward Bolton Priory.

2. After a short while, you come to another wooden gate. Go through the gate and follow the path round to the left. You will see a ford and a wooden bridge. Cross over the stream (you choose which way) then head up a very steep hill for about twenty yards until veering off right along a gravel path (NOT up the main road).

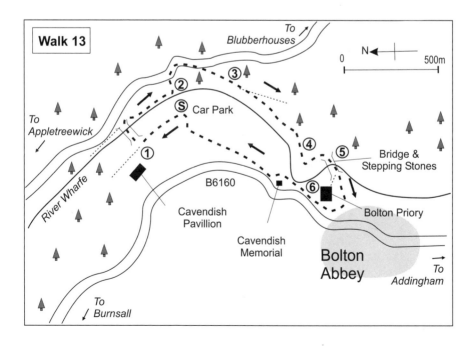

3. After a while you will come to a broken tree at either side of the path, which is full of coins. If you brought a coin, see if you can bang it into the tree.

   Keep to this path, passing over a very small waterfall. Soon, the path bends left (there is a wooden bench on the right of this corner). Shortly after this bend, the path forks. Take the right hand fork downwards, following the 'permissive footpath' sign. This is a very steep downhill section, followed by an uphill stretch of the same gradient.

4. At the end of the uphill stretch, Bolton Abbey Priory will just come into view. Head for the wooden gate and go though into the meadow. Walk downhill, with the river on your right.

   You will eventually come to a small sandy beach. This is a good place for skimming stones. Make sure you keep hold of one afterwards to take home and paint.

Bolton Abbey

At the beach, turn left and follow the path down towards the bridge. (NB: The stepping stones are deceiving – they look easy to cross, but are not with a toddler!).

5. Cross over the bridge and keep on the path for a few yards, then veer off right over the grass, heading towards the Abbey. When you get to a small wooden gate, go through and keep to the path with the Abbey on your right.

6. With the main entrance of the Abbey on your right, follow the path straight ahead towards another wooden gate (one large for vehicles, with a smaller one next to it). Go through the gate and keep tightly to the right hand side path, following it until you reach the stone fountain near the entrance to the car park. Follow this road back down to your car near the Cavendish Pavillion.

In The Area

You're totally spoiled for choice here. There's Hesketh Farm Park; which has farm animals to feed, smaller animals to pet, tractor rides, indoor and outdoor play areas and a café. (**www.heskethfarmpark.co.uk** Hesketh House, Bolton Abbey, BD23 6HA) Tel: 01756 710 444. It's around twenty pounds for a family of four, but is seasonal, so check opening times first.

Relativly newly open is The Yorkshire Dales Icecream Parlour; it has a great outdoor play area and a real 1950's retro style diner – with hot dogs, burgers and lots of icecream flavours (Calm Slate Farm, Halton East, Bolton Abbey, BD23 6EJ) **www.yorkshiredalesicecream.co.uk** Tel: 01756 710 685. The playground is free if you have bought food or drinks from the diner.

If you fancy a journey on a steam train, you can't get much better than **www.embsayboltonabbeyrailway.org.uk** (Bolton Abbey Station, Bolton Abbey, BD23 6AF). Tel: 01756 710 614. It's worth planning ahead as there are seasonal rides on offer e.g. Santa Express, Day Out with Thomas The Tank Engine etc…). Prices vary.

Walk 14: Lindley Wood Reservoir

A lovely, simple there-and-back stroll in the Washburn Valley – taking you alongside the reservoir to begin with, then through fields and eventually a great paddling stop at Dobb Park Bridge. The reservoir was built between 1869 and 1876 and has the capacity to hold 750 million gallons of water. Along the way are lots of blackberry bushes – so if you manage to save some (rather than eating them all) you can make some delicious blackberry muffins on your return home.

Distance	2.3 miles (3.7 km)
Allow	2 hours
Take with you	Bread for the ducks. Some Tupperware boxes to collect blackberries in, a towel for after paddling, magnifying glass
Getting there and parking	The reservoir is situated on the B6451 north of Otley. Park at the Otley side of the reservoir bridge. There isn't a car park – just a small area enough for a couple of cars in front of a metal gate
Map	Ordnance Survey Explorer 297
Grid Reference	209498
Post walk activity	Making Blackberry and banana muffins (see Activity 14 on page 120)

Once parked, go over the little stile next to the metal gate and with the reservoir on your right, keep straight to this footpath for a fair while.

1. Eventually, you will come to a bridge on the right. Cross over this (the River Washburn) and you will see a stone stile. Go over the stone stile into the field and keep walking with the wall on your right.

   After a while you will come to a wooden kissing gate. Go through this and keep to the path again.

   A little bit further on through the kissing gate is old tree trunks which is hollow at the base – a great place for hide and seek or a den. There are also some big blackberry bushes around here.

2. When the path comes to a fork, take the left fork towards a wooden stile. Go over the stile and you will come to the shallow ford and a very picturesque stone bridge (Dobb Park Bridge). This is a lovely

Looking back toward the bridge at Lindley Wood Reservoir

Lindley Reservoir Checklist

Spot

☐ Molehill
☐ Holly
☐ Nettles
☐ Ducks
☐ Water Inspection Point (WO) (AV)
☐ 3-arch bridge
☐ Cow pat

Feel

Gorse bush – how prickly does it feel? Are the flowers prickly too? Did you know that some gorse flowers are edible? They can be used in salads or even tea! It is also high in protein and as a result, is given to some livestock in winter when there is less greenery available

Magnify

Lichen on a dry stone wall. It looks a bit like bright yellow circular patches. Did you know there are approximately 2,271 species of lichens in the UK? It can be found on walls, pavements, trees and even the roof of your own house. Some lichen are used in medicines such as antibiotics. In arctic regions it can be a vital source of food for animals and, in ancient times, lichen was even used for packaging to protect Egyptian mummies! (NB: The Yorkshire Dales National Park Authority are working on conservation of moss and lichen on dry stone walls as it is an important part of the eco system – so be careful to just look and not touch)

Collect

Blackberries, to make muffins with when you get home

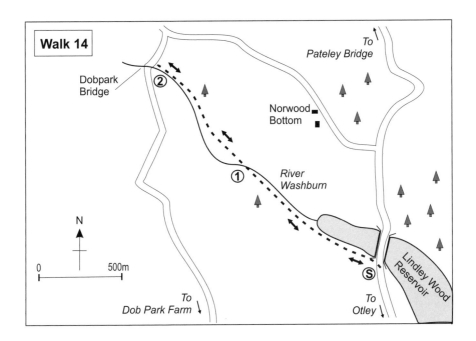

place to picnic or just rest while the children paddle. It is also the half way point.

Once you have splashed about and had a nibble, turn back the way you came (over the wooden stile) and just follow exactly the same route back.

In The Area

Lindley Wood Reservoir is just five miles out of Harrogate, where you will find lots to do.

Valley Gardens is a favourite of ours as it has a fantastic adventure playground, crazy golf, table tennis, a skateboard park, paddling pool and often extra things like bouncy castles and face painting in peak season. There is no charge for the park, but a small hire charge for the crazy golf etc. (**www.harrogate.gov.uk** Valley Gardens, Harrogate, HG2 0JH) tel: 01423 500 600.

Or RHS Garden, Harlow Carr is also well worth a visit (**www.rhs.org.uk/Gardens/Harlow-Carr**, Crag Lane, Harrogate, HG3 1UE) tel: 0845 265 8070. As well as the stunning gardens, there's a new adventure playground, a maze, treasure hunts, bird hide, café, shops etc. At the time of writing, a family of four could get in for £22.30.

Walk 15: Middleton Woods, Ilkley

This walk is best done in spring – early May sees the arrival of thousands of bluebells in the woods. It literally looks like the ground has been covered in a soft blue carpet and smells divine. If you look carefully, hiding among the trees and Great Bittercress, three types of butterfly are resident here; the Comma (noticeable for the white marking on its underwings, resembling a comma), the Tortoiseshell

Distance	0.9 miles (1.4 km)
Allow	1 hour
Take with you	Magnifying glass, bag or box to keep flower safe before pressing at home
Getting there and parking	At the traffic lights on the A65 in the centre of Ilkley turn down the hill (right if you are heading in the direction of Skipton). Follow the road down over the river and text the next turning on the right (back road to Otley). Park in the lay-by opposite the big green iron bridge
Map	Ordnance Survey Explorer 297
Grid Reference	122485
Post walk activity	Make a twig photo frame (see Avtivity 15 on page 120)

(with its dark body, red and yellow wings and a row of blue dots around the edge), and the Peacock (mainly rusty red, with a distinctive black, blue and yellow eye-spot at each wing tip). If you want to rest along the way to take in the scenery, there are a few bench stops, but no picnic tables.

On the opposite side of the road to the bridge, you should see a big wooden gate and a metal kissing gate – go through the gate and you will see a 'Welcome to Middleton Woods' sign. Here, the path forks – take the right hand path heading upwards. There is a slight fork a little later on (more of a veering off to the left) – just ignore this and keep straight on the main path.

1. As the path heads up, you will see a bench in front of you. Go left here. Soon you will cross a (very small) stream with some rocks through it. Then head up and right, passing a bench on your left.

2. You will get to another small stream with a rocky path through/over it. Go through/over this and carry on. Not long after

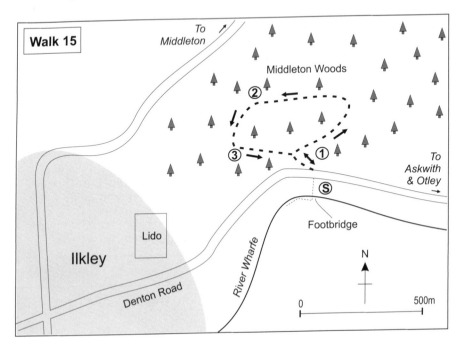

Emma in the bluebells at Middleton Woods

Middleton Woods Checklist

Spot

- ☐ Wooden bench
- ☐ Spider
- ☐ Sycamore tree
- ☐ Woodlouse
- ☐ Nettles
- ☐ Holly
- ☐ A bog (not toilet!)
- ☐ Fern
- ☐ Fungus
- ☐ Stream

Feel

The trunk of a sycamore tree. What does the bark feel like? Does it feel shiny and smooth or rough and jagged? It is actually one of the most widespread trees in this country – brought here centuries ago from mainland Europe. The oldest recorded sycamore tree in England is over three hundred years old and can be found in Dorset

Magnify

Woodlouse. You will most likely find one in the midst of a pile of leaves, under a stone or near a rotting log. Did you know that woodlouse have fourteen legs? They also have two antennae and a hard body armour-like shell to protect them from predators. Their favourite food is old leaves

Collect

One bluebell (for flower pressing)

this the path forks (well, it looks more like a woodland spaghetti junction). Take the left, lower fork (a small path) and follow the curve round to the left as though you are almost heading back.

3. The path soon goes downwards quite steeply, passing over a stream on a couple of wooden planks. Keep following the path down to the left. Eventually you will be back at the beginning, where you will spot the 'Middleton Woods' sign and the gate.

In The Area

Ilkley town centre has plenty of cafés, shops and a great park. Or if the weather isn't great, you could go to Ilkley Toy Museum (**www.ilkleytoymuseum.co.uk** Whitton Croft Road, Ilkley, LS29 9HR) tel: 01943 603 855. It contains one of the finest private collections of toys in the North of England. A family ticket is around eight pounds. Opening times are restricted, so please check to avoid disappointment. Or, if you're still feeling energetic, Ilkley Swimming Pool is nearby (with Lido in the summer), where you can also book tennis courts. (**www.bradford.gov.uk/bmdc/leisure_and_culture/ sports_and_leisure/sports_facilities/ilkley.htm**, Denton Road, Ilkley, LS29 0BZ) tel: 01943 600 453. A family of four could swim for around fifteen pounds (cheaper with a passport to leisure), but do check for opening times beforehand.

Activity 1: Edible sheep

After a fun walk in the countryside it is time to recharge the batteries with a tasty treat. These novelty cupcakes encourage kids to get involved with the baking and they taste fantastic too. They also allow the kids to make and discuss something they have seen on their walk as Dentdale is renowned for its fields of sheep.

What you need

On your walk
Have a look at the sheep while you are walking and talk through there features (fluffy coat, black face) with your kids.

From your kitchen

Utensils
12 Hole cupcake tin
12 Paper cupcake cases
1 Large and 1 small bowl
Wooden spoon
Kitchen scales
Sieve

Ingredients
100g Self raising flour
100g Butter or margarine
100g Caster sugar
2 Large eggs
Finely grated rind of 1 orange or lemon

For the decoration
50g Butter or margarine
100g Icing sugar
Freshly squeezed lemon or orange juice
Small marshmallows
Chocolate buttons, giant and normal size
Chocolate flakes

Plain cupcakes can be purchased from most supermarkets if you do not have time to cook the cakes yourself.

What to do

To make the cupcakes

Preheat the oven to 190oC (Gas mark 5). Place the cupcake cases into the holes of the cake tin.

Cream together the butter and the caster sugar, in a large bowl, until it is light and fluffy. Add the eggs one at a time and beat thoroughly.

Sieve the flour into the bowl and fold into the mixture, along with the lemon or orange zest.

Divide the mixture between the 12 cake cases and bake in the oven 15-20 mins until firm. Once cooked remove from the tin and cool on a rack.

To decorate

Cream the butter in a small bowl and sieve in the icing sugar a spoonful at a time. A teaspoon full of lemon or orange juice can be added for flavour (optional). Apply the butter icing to cover the top of each of the cupcakes. Save a little icing for making the eyes.

Place a giant chocolate button on one side of the cupcake and cut a standard chocolate button in half and position above for the ears. Cut the marshmallows in half and place across the cupcake so that it resembles a fluffy sheep!

To make the eyes place two small dots of white icing onto the chocolate button and top with a chocolate flake.

Activity 2: Leaf collage

Fallen leaves of many different shapes and sizes can be collected whilst out walking in the countryside. Competitions to find the biggest leaf, the funniest shape or the brightest colour all add to the excitement. However, don't just discard those leaves once you return to your car, take them home instead and the kids can make some fantastic collages.

What you need

On your walk
Collect as many different leaves as you can. Lots of different shapes, colours and sizes will add to the fun. Dry leaves are best as these can then be used straight away without any need for drying.

From your craft drawer
A4 paper (or larger) in any colour
Glue (white PVA is best, not pritstick)

Glue stick for spreading
Googly eyes (these bring animal pictures to life!)
Crayons

What to do

These are so many different possibilities for the design of your collage. It could be based on an animal (hedgehog, dinosaur.....), plant (trees, flowers.....), buildings, vehicles, this list is endless. Or you can just have fun making different patterns and textures.

Either spread the glue on the paper and stick the leaves to it or apply the glue directly to the leaves then place them on the paper in your chosen pattern. Crayons, eyes and any other crafting items you have at home can be used to enhance the collage as desired.

Allow to dry and then display!

Activity 3: Decorated eggs

Decorating eggs can be done at any time of the year but is especially fun at Easter time when they can be made into Easter chicks or bunnies. Alternatively, a range of different craft materials can be used to make fun paint textures or patterns.

What you need

On your walk

Eggs (these can be from your pantry or purchased whilst out and about! There is a farm selling eggs on the return leg of the Masham walk (Walk 3) but don't forget to take some money with you if you wish to buy some).

From your craft drawer
Paint - lots of colours
String
Bubble wrap
Rubber bands
Ribbon
Glue
Eyes, pom poms etc

What to do

Boil the eggs for 10 minutes and then remove them from the water and allow to cool.

Once cooled enough to handle remove the eggs from the water and allow to dry.

There are many different ways of decorating the egg:

1. Paint the pattern of your choice freehand.

2. Dip string in different coloured paint and drag them across the egg to make coloured patterns.

3. Place rubber bands around the egg to form a pattern then dip the egg whatever colour paint you choose. Allow to dry and remove the bands to reveal your patterned egg.

4. Coat the textured side of bubble wraps with paint and roll your egg across it to reveal a cool spotty pattern!

So choose which method you prefer, paint your egg, allow to dry and then embellish with ribbons, pom poms, googly eggs...........

Activity 4: Chalk drawing

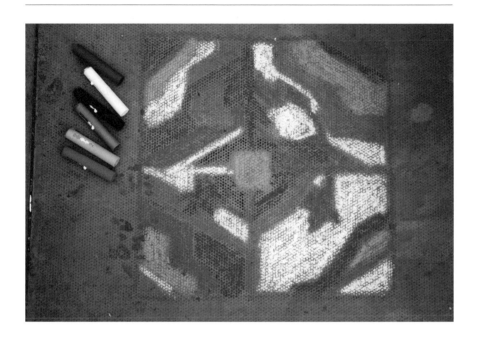

Chalk drawing is a great activity which can bring children and adults together in a joint experience. It is nice to sit down after a walk and talk about where you went and what you saw. Find a good spot in the garden and use chalk drawing to bring that walk back to life by drawing maps, animals, flowers and any other features you recall.

What you need

Chalk in a variety of sizes and colours. Soft chalk pastels (can be obtained from any art shop) are the best as the colours are very vibrant.
Clean street surface, step or paving slab.
Hand wipes
A cushion to sit on.
Sun hats and sun cream – it is easy to lose track of time!

What to do

Clean off an area of paving etc., get the chalks out and simply have a go. Here are a few pointers to get you started.

Talk about the colours that you have seen along the way and use those colours to build up patterns.

Outlines of animals and flowers can be drawn by adults and then coloured in by the kids.

The walks can be split in to sections and a story board created through drawings.

Activity 5: Conkers

Conkers has been played in Great Britain for generations and is a free and simple game that will amuse the kids for days! Below are the basic requirements and rules but more advanced rules for the serious players can be found on the internet (http://en.wikipedia.org/wiki/Conkers).

What you need

On your walk
If you find a horse chestnut tree along your route during the months of September and October then collect a bag full of conkers. Select the large even shaped ones that have no cracks or chips on them.

From your craft drawer
String

What to do

Make a hole through the middle of your chosen conker. Thread a piece of strong string, around 25cm in length, through the conker and secure with a knot at one end. You are now ready to play.

The game proceeds with two players taking it in turns to attempt to hit their opponent's conker.

One player must wrap their string around their hand and, keeping very still, allow the conker to hang on its string while it is used as a target!

The striker wraps their conker string around one hand, takes the conker in their other hand and draws it back ready for the strike. The conker is then aimed and released to attempt a strike. If the striker misses on the first strike two further attempts are allowed.

The game continues until one of the conkers is completely destroyed.

Activity 6: Stone Bugs

Painted pebbles make great paperweights or garden decorations and they make perfect presents too! They can even be used for playing games e.g. why not paint a number of small pebbles in two designs and then you could play a variation of noughts and crosses.

What you need

On your walk
Pick up a smooth pebble about the size of a bar of soap. Oval pebbles are perfect.

From your craft drawernts in a variety of colours
Paint brushes of various sizes (small ones are great to add details)
Spray varnish (optional; can be obtained from any good craft shop)
Stick on eyes (optional; great for making bug rocks!)
Felt
Glue
Scissors

What to do

Give your pebble a good clean in soapy water and then leave it to dry.

Plan your design, here are a couple of ideas to help you on your way:-

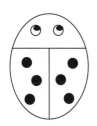

Ladybird

First paint the front third of your rock black and the rear two thirds red. Once this paint is dry add a black line through the red section to resemble wings and then add the black spots. Glue the eyes onto the black paint at the front of the pebble.

Bumble Bee

Paint your rock yellow and then allow to dry. Next add the black stripes across the main body of the rock. Glue two eyes to the front of the bee. Cut out two black felt wings and glue onto the top of the rock.

Once you have painted your design leave it to dry for a few hours. Now you can spray your pebble evenly with varnish (best for a grown up to do this bit) and this will prevent the painting from coming off. Once the varnish is dry adorn your pebble with eyes, felt or any extras you want to add.

If you wish to make it into a paperweight cut a piece of felt to the appropriate size and glue to the base of the rock.

Activity 7: Pine cone bird feeder

A quick but messy activity which brings weeks of enjoyment for all the family. Once the feeder is in the garden see how many different species of birds visit. Which species are the most regular visitors and which are your favourites?

What you need

On your walk
Pine cones. Large cones with large gaps between the scales are the best.

From your craft drawer
String
Lard
Bird seed

What to do

Tie the string around the widest part of the cone and secure in place with a knot. Make sure the knot is nice and tight as the string is used to suspend the feeder from a branch.

Mix the lard and bird seed together and press it into the openings of the cone. This is the messy bit so make sure your table is protected and the kids have got their aprons on!

Hang the feeder in your garden and enjoy watching the birds feed.

Activity 8: Dinosaur footprints

The dinosaurs have been out walking in the Dales! Follow the trail of dinosaur footprints on your walk in Malham (Walk 8) and then why not have a go at making your own trail at home. These fun potato prints are easy to do and different sizes, shapes and colours can be used to represent different dinosaurs.

What you need

From your kitchen
Potatoes
Small knife (for adult use only)

From your craft drawer
Paint (a variety of colours)
Paper (a roll of paper allows you to make a long trail of footprints)
Paint brush

What to do

Cut your potato in half and carefully cut out a raised impression of a dinosaur foot print. Here is a template to help you on your way.

Once you have designed you footprint either dip the potato into a saucer of paint or use the brush to apply some paint to it and then press this onto your paper.

Make a trail of prints across the paper using different colours or sizes of prints to show different dinosaurs. Great big prints for T-rex and small ones for the sprightly Velociraptor!

Activity 9: Yorkshire rose flag

The White Rose is an important symbol of Yorkshire's history and dates back to the time of the war of the roses in the 15th Century. Learn about this symbol by taking a rubbing of the rose whilst on your walk and then using this to make a flag at home.

What you need

On your walk
Take a rubbing (see Activity 18 on page 127) of a Yorkshire Rose one of the benches at Saint Michael and all Angels Church on the Grassington walk (walk 9).

Collect a stick, suitable to attach to your flag whilst on your walk too.

From your craft drawer
Coloured pencils
Glue
Sticky tape

What to do
Take your Yorkshire Rose rubbing and colour in (as above). The rose should be white but the leaves can be coloured green and the background of the flag should be blue.

Attach the flag to your stick using either glue or sticky tape.

Proudly fly the flag at your leisure!

Activity 10: Krispie birds nests

Rice krispie cakes are always a favourite with the kids and are also very simple to make. These yummy treats are also filled with delicious eggs and look just like the birds nests we see when we are out walking. Aprons are definitely essential as this is a very sticky job!

What you need

On your walk
There are lots of different birds to be seen while out and about. Ducks are usually in abundance on walk 10 but there are also lots of song birds in the trees and if, you look closely, you may spot a few nests.

From your kitchen

Utensils
12 Hole cupcake tin
12 Paper cupcake cases
1 Large bowl
Wooden spoon
Kitchen scales

Ingredients
100g Rice krispies
100g Butter or margarine
100g Diary/Cream toffees
100g Marshmallows
Mini chocolate eggs or jelly beans

What to do

Place 12 cupcake cases into a bun tin.

Place the butter, toffees and marshmallows into a saucepan and heat gently. Keep stirring all the time until all the ingredients have melted and then boil for approximately 1 minute.

Remove the mixture from the heat and pour over the rice krispies. Stir the rice krispies until they are all evenly coated with the toffee mixture.

Divide the rice krispies between the cake cases making sure you leave a dip in the top of each nest ready for the eggs.

Fill each nest with chocolate eggs or jelly beans and leave the nests to set.

Activity 11: Cardboard Castle

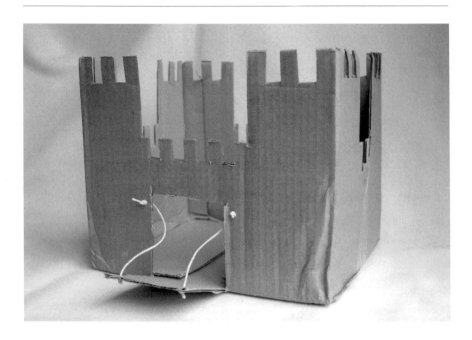

Castles are fun and mysterious places full of kings, queens and knights. These sites of battles and banquets are bound to trigger the imagination of any child so why not build a castle of your own so that the adventure can be continued at home! A castle can easily be created from a cardboard box and once decorated, can provide hours of fun and inventive play.

What you need

On your walk
Take a look at the structure and shape of Ripley Castle to gain inspiration for your own design.

From your craft drawer
A cardboard box (any size will do as it depends on how large you want your castle to be!)
Scissors (to be used be an adult)

String
Paint, pens or crayons (optional)

What to do

Cut the top flaps off the cardboard box so that you are left with a box with a base and four sides but no lid.

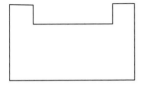

Remove a rectangle from the middle of the top of each side to leave a tower in each of the four corners.

Cut small rectangles out of the entire top edge of the box to form the battlements.

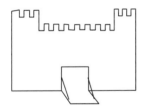

Cut a draw bridge into the front of the castle. Do not cut the bridge along the bottom of the box. Put two holes in the sides of the bridge and use string to attach these to the main box so forming the drawbridge.

Decorate your castle with paints, pens or crayons.

Activity 12: Clock face

Clocks of many different forms and shapes are a feature in many urban and rural environments but did you manage to spot the clock face on the Skipton Woods route (Walk 12)? Make your own clock face with this fun but educational activity that will help your child understand how to tell the time.

What you need

From your craft drawer
Paper plate
Coloured card
Number stickers (1-12)
Scissors
Brass paper fastener
Paint, pens or crayons (optional)

What to do

The paper plate is going to form the clock face. Colour or paint if desired.

Place the number stickers (or write on the numbers if you don't have stickers) in the appropriate locations on the clock face.

Draw two arrows on the coloured card. One should be larger than the other, and approximately the radius of the plate.

Push the blunt ends of the arrows onto the brass paper fastener and then push the fastener through the centre of the paper plate and fix in place (this should be loose enough to enable the clock hands to move). The clock is now ready to tell the time!

Activity 13: St George's flag collage

St George is the patron saint of England and is celebrated annually on the 23rd April. Legend says that St George slayed a dragon in order to save the King of Egypt's daughter from a terrible fate. St George's flag is usually seen flying on the flag pole at Bolton Abbey. Here is a fun way to make your own St Georges Cross which you can proudly display at home.

What you need

From your craft drawer
White card
Pencil
PVA glue
Red and white tissue paper

What to do

Take the card and draw a rectangular flag shape with a cross on it (as for St George's Flag) in pencil as a guide for your sticking.

Scrunch up lots of small pieces of red and white tissue paper.

Apply the PVA glue to the area inside the rectangle on your card. Stick the red tissue paper pieces to the cross and the white tissue paper to the rest of the rectangle.

Allow to dry and then display.

Activity 14:
Blackberry and banana muffins

Walking in late summer and early autumn is always a treat as the hedgerows are laden with juicy blackberries. If you manage to store some away before the kids devour them all then why not use them in this tasty recipe. These muffins are packed with fruit and oats and so make a healthy and wholesome treat.

What you need

From your walk
Whilst out on your walk make sure you collect a punnet of blackberries as you will need about 150g for this recipe.

From your kitchen

Utensils
12 Hole muffin tin
12 Paper muffin cases
1 Large and 1 small bowl
Wooden spoon
Kitchen scales
Sieve

Ingredients
300g Self raising flour
1tsp Bicarbonate of soda
100g Light brown sugar
50g Porridge oats (plus 1tbsp for the topping)
2 Medium sized ripe bananas
284ml Buttermilk
5tbsp Light olive oil
2 Egg whites

What to do

Preheat your oven to 180oC (Gas mark 4) and fill the holes in the muffin tin with the paper cases.

Sieve the flour and bicarbonate of soda into a large bowl.

Measure out the sugar and then reserve 1 tbsp for later use. Add the rest of the sugar and the oats to the flour and stir.

In a separate bowl mash the bananas with a fork until they are almost smooth. Add the buttermilk, oil and egg whites and mix thoroughly with the banana.

Make a well in the centre of the flour mix and pour in the banana mix. Stir quickly but sparingly with a wooden spoon until just combined (there should still be a few flecks of flour visible).

Add the blackberries and give the mix one final stir. Divide between the muffin cases (they should be almost full) and sprinkle the tops with the remaining sugar and oats.

Bake for 15-20 mins. The muffins should have risen and have dark golden tops.

Cool, eat and enjoy!

Activity 15: Twig photo frame

Exploring in the woods is always fun with so many places to hide, dens to build and nature to investigate. While you are there pick up a selection of small twigs and you can make this fantastic photo frame to display a photo of your fun day out or maybe a leaf collage (see Activity 2) made with leaves collected whilst you are there.

What you need

On your walk
You will need a selection of small twigs. 6-8 that are about 20 cm in length and 6-8 that are shorter (15 cm). Twigs of these lengths are appropriate for a standard 6x4 inch photo.

From your craft drawer
Twine, string or wool
Piece of cardboard approximately 1cm wider and 1cm longer than your photo.
Glue (hot glue works best but should only be used by an adult).

What to do

Take one bundle (3-4) of long twigs and one of short twigs and cross them over to form one of the corners of the frame. Tie the twigs together using twine in an 'X' pattern around the twigs.

Repeat this for the other 3 corners to form a rectangular frame. The space in the middle of the frame should be approximately the same size as your photograph.

Trim your piece of cardboard so that it is the same size as the frame and glue each corner and along the bottom. Stick to the frame. Gluing in the corners alone on the top of the frame will allow you to easily insert your art work and change it when desired whilst the glue along the bottom should prevent your art work or photo from falling out of the frame.

Make a twine loop at the top of the frame so that it can be hung on a wall.

Once the glue is dry you can insert your photo or art work into the frame.

Activity 16: How to play Poohsticks

This is a really fun game – made famous by the author A.A. Milne in his book *The House of Pooh Corner*.

Two or more people can play. It involves finding a stick of roughly equal length and width as that of the other players.

Then, standing on a bridge over running water, everybody drops their sticks down towards flowing water at the same time. The players then quickly turn to the other side and peer over the bridge.

The first stick to flow under the bridge is the winner.

NB: Make sure you agree which stick belongs to whom before you drop them so as to avoid arguments.

This game could also be played with leaves , bits of bark, anything which floats easily and could be carried along on a current.

Activity 17: Pond dipping

Pond dipping can be great fun for children as you never know what you might come across. There are minibeasts, insects, flatworms, water spiders, leeches, larvae, plants (and usually a few dead leaves...). But whatever you find, the point is that this activity is engaging your child in the natural environment – opening their mind to the fact that whole other worlds function in different surroundings.

As this activity is going to be done during a walk, I've kept the kit to a minimum:
A plastic container (about the size of an icecream tub)
A smaller container (about the size of a yogurt pot)
Magnifying Glass
Some wipes for your hands afterwards
A camera, so you can look up any fascinating creatures when you get home
Or a pen/pencil to record your findings

So, making sure you have a good hold on your little one, let them lean forward and dip the container into the pond at the edge – filling it about half full. Then move back away from the pond. Taking your smaller container, dip it in the larger one for a sample – this enables you to take a closer look.

Remember to treat all these minibeasts and pondlife with respect – don't touch them with your hands, just look with the magnifying glass or naked eye.

Then try to describe what you've found – if it's a creature, how many legs does it have? Does it look hairy or smooth? Does it look like a tiny fish?.. a tadpole?...Does it move around fast or slow?...Perhaps it's chasing after something else ?... Or is it some kind of plant-life? What colour is it?...Does it look like it has a stiff stem or just flows about in the water?...does it float near the surface or stay at the bottom of the pot?

At this stage, take some photos for identification when you get home. Or make a few notes about what you've seen.

When you have finished examining the water, gently pour it back into the pond, trying to make as little disturbance as possible.

Now, give your hands a very good clean with the wipes – and you're done. Don't forget to take your containers home with you – and enjoy looking up your findings when you return home. The library is always a useful source of information (or you can always look things up on the internet. I found **www.naturegrid.org.uk** quite helpful).

Activity 18: Crayon rubbings

The great thing about crayon rubbings is that you can use all sorts of surfaces and textures to create some really interesting patterns. Mix it up with different colours for added effect. Then you can keep them as pictures, cut them into small oblongs for bookmarks, stick them onto card for a home-made birthday card or why not cut them out to arrange in a collage? There are so many options.

All you need is a few crayons and some paper. Any colour paper will do, but try to contrast it with the crayon (i.e. if using darker paper, use lighter crayons).

To do a crayon rubbing
Find an interesting texture like the trunk of a tree, a wall, some engraving on stone or wood carvings.

Use one hand to hold the paper steady across the surface (or ask someone to hold it steady for you).

With your other hand gently, using the side of the crayon, rub it back and forth over the paper.

You will see the textures emerging.

Some surfaces look better with gentle crayon rubbing; others (such as inscriptions in stone) tend to work better if you press on harder.

Lifting the paper off the surface, then moving it slightly and rubbing again gives a denser pattern.

Also from Sigma:

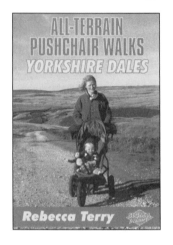